The Age of Romanticism

The Age of Romanticism

JOANNE SCHNEIDER

Greenwood Guides to Historic Events, 1500–1900
Linda S. Frey and Marsha L. Frey, Series Editors

GREENWOOD PRESS
Westport, Connecticut • London

Library of Congress Cataloging-in-Publication Data

Schneider, Joanne.
    The age of romanticism / Joanne Schneider.
        p. cm. — (Greenwood guides to historic events, 1500–1900, ISSN 1538-442X)
    Includes bibliographical references and index.
    ISBN 978-0-313-31764-4 (alk. paper)
    1. Romanticism in art. 2. Arts, European—18th century. 3. Arts, European—19th century. I. Title.
NX452.5.R64S36 2007
700.9′034—dc22   2007006559

British Library Cataloguing in Publication Data is available.

Library of Congress Catalog Card Number: 2007006559
ISBN-13: 978-0-313-31764-4
ISBN-10: 0-313-31764-X
ISSN: 1538-442X

First published in 2007

Greenwood Press, 88 Post Road West, Westport, CT 06881
An imprint of Greenwood Publishing Group, Inc.
www.greenwood.com

Printed in the United States of America

∞

The paper used in this book complies with the Permanent Paper Standard issued by the National Information Standards Organization (Z39.48–1984).

10 9 8 7 6 5 4 3 2 1

Copyright Acknowledgment

The author and the publisher gratefully acknowledge permission to use the following material:

Letter from *Caspar David Friedrich in Briefen und Bekenntnissen*, edited by Sigrid Hinz (Berlin: Henschelverlag, 1968). Used by permission of Seemann Henschel GmbH & Co. KG.

To my grandfather, my father, and my husband,
Rev. Thomas Anderson
Dr. Joseph Schneider
Mr. T. Arthur Bone
who by their example encouraged in me
intellectual curiosity, dedication to work, and a sense of humor

CONTENTS

Photographs follow page 76.

SERIES FOREWORD

American statesman Adlai Stevenson stated, "We can chart our future clearly and wisely only when we know the path which has led to the present." This series, Greenwood Guides to Historic Events, 1500–1900, is designed to illuminate that path by focusing on events from 1500 to 1900 that have shaped the world. The years 1500 to 1900 include what historians call the early modern period (1500 to 1789, the onset of the French Revolution) and part of the modern period (1789 to 1900).

In 1500, an acceleration of key trends marked the beginnings of an interdependent world and the posing of seminal questions that changed the nature and terms of intellectual debate. The series closes with 1900, the inauguration of the twentieth century. This period witnessed profound economic, social, political, cultural, religious, and military changes. An industrial and technological revolution transformed the modes of production, marked the transition from a rural to an urban economy, and ultimately raised the standard of living. Social classes and distinctions shifted. The emergence of the territorial and later the national state altered man's relations with and view of political authority. The shattering of the religious unity of the Roman Catholic world in Europe marked the rise of a new pluralism. Military revolutions changed the nature of warfare. The books in this series emphasize the complexity and diversity of the human tapestry and include political, economic, social, intellectual, military, and cultural topics. Some of the authors focus on events in U.S. history such as the Salem witchcraft trials, the American Revolution, the abolitionist movement, and the Civil War. Others analyze European topics, such as the Reformation and Counter-Reformation and the French Revolution. Still others bridge cultures and continents by examining the voyages of discovery, the Atlantic slave trade, and the Age of Imperialism. Some focus on intellectual questions that have shaped the modern world, such as Charles Darwin's *Origin of Species*, or on turning points such as the Age of Romanticism. Others examine defining economic, religious, or legal events or issues such as the building of the railroads, the Second Great Awakening, and abolitionism. Heroes (e.g., Meriwether Lewis and William Clark), scientists (e.g., Darwin), military leaders (e.g., Napoleon Bonaparte), poets (e.g., Lord Byron) stride across the pages. Many of these events were seminal in that they marked profound changes or turning points. The Scientific Revolution, for example, changed the way individuals viewed themselves and their world.

The authors, acknowledged experts in their fields, synthesize key events, set developments within the larger historical context, and, most important, present well-balanced, well-written accounts that integrate the most recent scholarship in the field.

The topics were chosen by an advisory board composed of historians, high school history teachers, and school librarians to support the curriculum and meet student research needs. The volumes are designed to serve as resources for student research and to provide clearly written interpretations of topics central to the secondary school and lower-level undergraduate history curriculum. Each author outlines a basic chronology to guide the reader through often-confusing events and presents a historical overview to set those events within a narrative framework. Three to five topical chapters underscore critical aspects of the event. In the final chapter the author examines the impact and consequences of the event. Biographical sketches furnish background on the lives and contributions of the players who strut across the stage. Ten to fifteen primary documents, ranging from letters to diary entries, song lyrics, proclamations, and posters, cast light on the event, provide material for student essays, and stimulate critical engagement with the sources. Introductions identify the authors of the documents and the main issues. In some cases a glossary of selected terms is provided as a guide to the reader. Each work contains an annotated bibliography of recommended books, articles, CD-ROMs, Internet sites, videos, and films that set the materials within the historical debate.

Reading these works can lead to a more sophisticated understanding of the events and debates that have shaped the modern world and can stimulate a more active engagement with the issues that still affect us. It has been a particularly enriching experience to work closely with such dedicated professionals. We have come to know and value even more highly the authors in this series and our editors at Greenwood, particularly Kevin Ohe and Michael Hermann.

In many cases they have become more than colleagues; they have become friends. To them and to future historians we dedicate this series.

Linda S. Frey
University of Montana

Marsha L. Frey
Kansas State University

PREFACE

"Romanticism was by its very nature provisional: it reacted against what lay around it, was constantly mutating, and was often defined by what it was not."[1] Can something that is constantly mutating be defined and discussed easily? Obviously not. Nevertheless, the historian's task involves sifting through the evidence of the past in order to write its story and more importantly interpret its relevance for today. The Age of Romanticism and the people associated with it have assumed legendary proportions. To understand their historical importance, it is critical to reach beyond the myths to the events, people, and legacy of this fascinating era.

Such a process must begin with definitions. How does one define Romanticism or Romantic?[2] Noted scholars suggest one cannot speak of Romanticism, but of Romanticisms, because Romantic artists' values differed according to nationality, gender, and time period.[3] Despite the wide variation, certain common themes pervade the Romantic era: a cult of emotion, a stress on the imagination, the importance of personal feelings, an almost religious-like attachment to nature, a fascination with the exotic, a rejection of progress in Western civilization and a nostalgia for the past, and suspicion of uniformity at the expense of individuality. Romantics also believed in the personal and intuitive truth, the emphasis on man's spiritual side, and the important role writers, painters, and musicians had in bringing those concepts together through their works.

The Age of Romanticism involves events in Europe from approximately 1770 to 1880. Romantic writers, artists, and musicians can be found throughout the world, but this overview focuses on German, British, and French Romanticism with brief mention of Italian and Russian.

Chapter 1, "Overview: The Eighteenth-Century Antecedents," describes the political, social, and intellectual milieu out of which Romanticism emerges.

Chapter 2, "'Minutes of Active Sensitivity': Romantic Poetry," revisits Great Britain's poets and then proceeds to the Continent to explore select German, Italian, and Russian poets and their works.

Chapter 3, "Romantic Prose and Drama," investigates fairy tales, novellas, novels, and dramas associated with the era. After introducing the genres, it describes select authors, grouped by nationality.

Chapters 4 and 5, "Romantic Painting" and "The Most Romantic Art: Music," chronicle the continuities and discontinuities from Classical to Romantic styles in art and music, and discuss select practitioners.

Chapter 6, "Romantic Legacies," describes how issues associated with Romanticism, nationalism and environmentalism, have continued to be a part of contemporary Western civilization's intellectual heritage.

Biographical sketches of key figures, primary source document excerpts, and a selected bibliography will enhance the reader's understanding of this era.

Notes

1. David Blayney Brown, *Romanticism* (New York: Phaidon, 2001), 8.

2. An informative, but dated (1943), discussion of Romanticism's definitions appears in Jacques Barzun, *Classic, Romantic, and Modern* (Chicago: University of Chicago Press, 1975), 1–17, 155–168.

3. The original argument concerning Romanticisms comes from A. O. Lovejoy's talk at the 1923 Modern Language Association meeting, "On the Discrimination of Romanticisms." Reprinted in his *Essays on the History of Ideas* (New York: George Braziller, 1955), 228–253. The debate continues, with reference to Lovejoy and others who over the decades have discussed this issue. Please consult Christoph Bode, "Europe," in *Romanticism: An Oxford Guide*, ed. Nicholas Roe (New York: Oxford University Press, 2005), 126–136.

ACKNOWLEDGMENTS

Although writing a book is a solitary experience, the end product is affected by the aid of others. I would like to especially thank my colleagues Karl Benziger, J. Stanley Lemons, Mary Lucas, Ann Marie Kordas, and the late Nancy Norton for the time they took to comment on and help me improve this book. My husband Arthur Bone, countless friends, family members, colleagues, and students must also be thanked for putting up with my questions and comments about the labors involved in this effort. I would also like to thank series editors Linda Frey and Marsha Frey for their encouraging and helpful commentary.

CHRONOLOGY OF EVENTS

1757	Edmund Burke publishes *Philosophical Enquiry into the Origins of Our Ideas on the Sublime and the Beautiful*.
1761	Jean-Jacques Rousseau's *Julie, or The New Eloise* appears.
1762	Rousseau's *Émile* and *The Social Contract* are published.
1767	The *Sturm und Drang* (Storm and Stress) literary movement in Germany begins. Its writers express the same criticisms about society as do the later Romantics. It ends around 1785.
1774	Johann Wolfgang von Goethe's *The Sorrows of Young Werther* is published.
1781	Rousseau's *Confessions* creates a stir.
1789	William Blake publishes *Songs of Innocence*.
1789, May	The Estates General convenes.
1789, June	The members of the Third Estate of the Estates General establish the National Assembly.
1789, July	Parisians storm the royal fortress, known as the Bastille, and conquer it.
1790	Burke publishes *Reflections on the Revolution in France*.
1792, April	The War of the First Coalition begins against France. It continues until 1797.
1793, January	Execution of King Louis XVI occurs.

1793, July	The Reign of Terror begins and continues until late July 1794.
	Blake's *Songs of Experience* and Ann Radcliffe's *The Mysteries of Udolfo* are published.
1795	The Directory takes charge of France and continues the war with Europe.
	Goethe's *Wilhelm Meister's Years of Apprenticeship* is published.
1798	Publication of Wordsworth's and Coleridge's *Lyrical Ballads* occurs. (The "Preface" is appended to the 1800 edition.)
	Friedrich and August Wilhelm Schlegel begin publication of the literary journal *The Athenaeum*, which continues for two years.
1799	The Directory collapses and is replaced by The Consulate. Napoleon becomes first consul and eventually eliminates the other two consuls.
1803	Beethoven's symphony *Eroica* is completed.
1804	Napoleon names himself Emperor.
1806	Sydney Owenson, Lady Morgan's *The Wild Irish Girl* appears.
1808	Goethe completes *Faust Part I*; Felicia Hemans publishes *Poems*; and Fichte's *Addresses to the German Nation* appears.
1810	Madame de Staël's *Germany* is secretly published in Paris and Wordsworth writes "Topographical Description of the Country of the Lakes," which appears anonymously in Joseph Wilkinson's *Select Views of Cumberland*.
1812	Lord Byron's *Childe Harold's Pilgrimage* Parts I and II appear.
	Napoleon invades Russia and is eventually forced to retreat in October.
1813	Shelley publishes *Queen Mab*. Coalition mobilizes against Napoleon.

1814	After Napoleon's initial surrender, he is sent to the island of Elba, off the west coast of Italy. Louis XVIII assumes the French throne.
	Sir Walter Scott's *Waverley* appears anonymously.
1815	Napoleon returns to Paris for the One Hundred Days. Europe's political leaders, meeting at the Congress of Vienna, respond to his threat. Napoleon and his forces are defeated at the Battle of Waterloo in June. Napoleon abdicates and is then sent to St. Helena, a barren island in the south Atlantic.
1816	Lord Byron leaves England and that summer writes Part III of *Childe Harold's Pilgrimage*, which discusses Napoleon.
	Coleridge publishes *Biographia Literaria*.
1818	Anonymous publication of Mary Shelley's *Frankenstein* and Jane Austen's *Northanger Abbey* occurs.
1819	Showing of Géricault's *Raft of the Medusa* meets with less than enthusiastic reception in Paris.
1820	Lord Byron publishes *Don Juan*, John Keats "Endymion," and Percy Bysshe Shelley *Prometheus Unbound*.
1821	John Constable exhibits *The Hay Wain*.
1822	Shelley drowns off the coast of Italy mid-summer.
1823	Franz Schubert composes *The Unfinished Symphony*.
1824	Lord Byron travels to Greece to aid in its war with Turkey and dies there.
	Beethoven's Ninth Symphony receives an ecstatic reception.
1826	Delacroix paints *The Death of Sardanapalus*.
1827	Victor Hugo publishes "The Preface" to *Cromwell* in which he defines Romantic drama.
1830, July	A revolution forces King Charles X of France from the throne. To mark the event Delacroix paints *Liberty Leading the People*.

	Hector Berlioz's *Symphonie fantastique* is completed.
1832	George Sand publishes *Indiana*.
1837	Aleksandr Pushkin is killed in a duel at age 38.
1842	Alessandro Manzoni rewrites *The Betrothed* in the Tuscan dialect to promote it as the national language of Italy.
1843	Wordsworth becomes Poet Laureate of Britain.
1848, February	The citizens of France revolt against their king. Then capitals in eastern and southern Europe erupt in revolutionary movements, which last until late 1849.
1876	Wagner's complete *Ring of the Nibelungen* is performed at the Bayreuth Festival Hall for the first time.

CHAPTER 1

OVERVIEW: THE EIGHTEENTH-CENTURY ANTECEDENTS

The Age of Romanticism stands at an important divide in the history of Western civilization. From 1750 on, economic and social changes associated with the beginnings of industrial manufacturing unleashed forces that would affect where people lived and how they earned a living. Ideas associated with the Scientific Revolution and the Enlightenment produced questions about the monopoly of political power, which traditionally had rested with European kings and the nobility, and the resulting social inequalities. Such challenges eventually led to the two great political upheavals of the late eighteenth century, the American Revolution (1776–1783) and the French Revolution (1789–1799). Against this backdrop, the intellectuals associated with Romanticism developed their aesthetic theories and created works of art that responded to their world.

At a quick glance, it appears that the Enlightenment, with its emphasis on rationalism, and Romanticism, with its stress on emotions, are diametrically opposed. This contrast oversimplifies what is a much more complex interrelationship. The Enlightenment did not totally abandon emotion, nor did the Romantic era reject rationalism. Within the Enlightenment critique the first notions associated with Romanticism appear. The overlap of these two traditions can be better understood by examining the life and work of two important eighteenth-century intellectuals, associated primarily with the Enlightenment, whose ideas foreshadow Romanticism.

The complexity of Jean-Jacques Rousseau's (1712–1778) life and thought cannot be thoroughly discussed here. His ties with Enlightenment traditions rest in his belief in the innate goodness of humanity and his idea that a social contract among consenting individuals can lead to a well-ordered and fair world. His unconventional life gave him a far different perspective on the world than that of other *philosophes*. In his first major publication, *Discourse on the Sciences and the Arts* (1750), he rejected the idea that contemporary civilization and its advances had made the world better. He believed man's nature is naturally good and that civilization corrupts the individual. He also disliked the excessive optimism and emphasis on reason that dominated Enlightenment thought.

Rousseau's writings include original musical scores, intellectual treatises, novels, and his famous autobiography. Two selections in particular connect him to the Age of Romanticism: the novel *Julie, or The New Eloise* (1761) and his autobiography, *Confessions* (1781–1788). In the novel, the heroine, Julie, falls in love with the wrong man, but after a brief affair, she marries the acceptable older man—the one approved of by both family and the larger society. She attempts to be a good wife and mother but eventually recognizes she is still in love with the young man. She accepts her passion but does not yield to it; she dies after saving one of her children from drowning. The novel warns that an individual's feelings should not be suppressed and that everyone needs to recognize the importance of self instead of conforming to what society considers proper.[1]

Rousseau's *Confessions*, tame reading today, shocked the eighteenth-century world. (See Primary Document 1.) He placed himself at center stage and described his rather irregular lifestyle, which included theft, adulterous affairs, and illegitimate children. Rousseau believed himself to be unique but also saw himself as a spokesman for all humanity.[2] Some critics claim the *Confessions* inaugurated the Romantic era because this best seller not only introduces the concept of the "self" but also such ideas as rejection of the city and the praise of solitude. Rousseau calls on "wild nature" to serve as a source of inspiration. All these themes appear in subsequent Romantic writing, painting, and music.[3]

No one could be more opposite to Rousseau than Edmund Burke (1729–1797), who also played a transitional role between Enlightenment and Romantic thought. Most people know Burke because of his impassioned critique of the French Revolution, *Reflections on the Revolution in France* (1790), but earlier, he had written about art. In 1756, Burke wrote *Philosophical Enquiry into the Origins of Our Ideas on the Sublime and the Beautiful* (1757). He attacked rationalism and the rigid Classicism of the eighteenth-century artistic style, which emphasized balance, harmony, and restraint. Burke believed the greatest thing about art is its ability to depict the Infinite: that which knows no limits. He felt poetry could accomplish this better than prose or painting. He suggested art must reach a person's imagination and, through it, the passions. Burke discussed two important artistic concepts: the sublime and the beautiful.[4] Burke wrote less about beauty and the beautiful than he did about the sublime. In his discussion, he dismissed Enlightenment views, which looked to Ancient Greek and Roman statues for a depiction of beauty. In his view, Classical art forms appeal too much to reason. He suggested beauty should be associated with the image of the "ideal woman" and the softer virtues of compassion and kindness. Still, for him, the love that beauty evokes is a less important passion than the awe which the sublime inspires. (See Primary Document 2.)[5]

Both Rousseau's and Burke's names are linked to the 1789 French Revolution, which destroyed *ancien régime* society and challenged the Enlightenment's rationalistic optimism. Many revolutionaries claimed Rousseau's writings inspired them to confront the inequalities and injustices of their world. At the same time, the revolution's opponents rallied to Burke and his condemnation of this revolution in particular and all radical challenges to established society in general.

While Rousseau and Burke served as precursors to Romanticism, a contemporary group of German writers also balked at the Enlightenment's overly rational orientation. Collectively known as the *Sturm und Drang* (Storm and Stress [1767–1785]), these writers endorsed the Enlightenment's rational efforts at political and social reform, yet they rejected its spirit. Like Rousseau, they denied the Enlightenment's optimistic view that contemporary civilization continued to progress. They glorified nature, which the *philosophes* had treated as an object of scientific study. They rejected the enlightened ideal of rational, critical man in favor of the original genius who lived as a free, "natural" person, unhindered by the expectations, rules, and conventions of "civilized" society. They admired innocent children, naïve women, peasants, craftsmen, and simple people of earlier times. They acknowledged the individual's irrational side and explored matters of the heart and concepts like feeling, sentiment, and motivation. The contrast between the self's apparently limited capacities and potentially limitless possibilities fascinated them as well.[6]

Moreover, the *Sturm und Drang* writers wished to break from the rules of the eighteenth-century intellectual world with its elite men of letters and to allow creativity to flourish. They rejected the dominance of French style within the literary world and sought creative genius within German culture. They believed that insight could be found among folk songs and the stories passed on orally within peasant households. Interestingly enough, this search for cultural roots actually began in Britain with the publication of several books in the 1760s, which highlighted earlier folk traditions, and then continued in the German lands.[7]

Like the subsequent Romantics, the *Sturm und Drang* writers wanted to use "authentic" language in their works. This involved rejecting the formal literary language dictated by Classical cultural norms in favor of a simpler style. Their poetry consisted of free verse, which seemed to grow organically rather than emerge from a set of prescribed rules. They resurrected the ballad, a medieval literary style, and legitimated the language of folk songs. Through their dramas, *Sturm und Drang* authors addressed the problem of natural man's conflict with established society. They investigated themes such as the battle for political freedom, the wars of liberation against oppressive rulers, the fight for true love despite social class differences, the exposure of society's questionable morals, and the conflict between organized religion and man's more primitive, unsullied "natural" beliefs.[8]

The best-known piece of *Sturm und Drang* literature was Johann Wolfgang von Goethe's *The Sorrows of Young Werther* (1774). The novel tells the story of a young, sensitive man who has fallen in love with a married woman. The hero is a misfit who can find no happiness in polite society. He is only content when he spends time with children and simple folk. Even nature cannot help him overcome his pain, and he eventually kills himself. (See Primary Document 3.) The tragedy of the isolated, misunderstood, often love-struck hero frequently reappears in Romantic literature.

Goethe (1749–1832), Germany's greatest author, served as a godfather to the Age of Romanticism. *The Sorrows of Young Werther* provided a hero who became an archetype for Romantic authors. Many of them identified with Werther because they believed that an artist's true potential cannot be realized unless he has truly experienced love. Not only did the novel prefigure much Romantic prose and poetry, but Goethe corresponded with those individuals associated with the University of Jena, a birthplace of German Romanticism. Goethe's *Wilhelm Meister's Years of Apprenticeship* (1796) became a favorite among the Romantics because it not only told the story of a young genius and his education, but also because the text itself contained prose, poetry, and scientific discussions. This irregularity was exciting because Goethe had produced a work that broke genre rules.[9]

Goethe's great friend and collaborator, Friedrich Schiller (1759–1805), although regarded as a Classical author, nevertheless shared aesthetic perspectives with the Romantics. Schiller connects with them through his views about the problems the individual faces in modern society and where the artist fits in that scenario. Schiller, like the English Romantics Wordsworth and Shelley, sees the writer or artist as having the ability because of an enhanced imagination to understand modern tensions and then through art bring reconciliation to mankind. Schiller expanded his ideas in *On Naïve and Sentimental Poetry* (1795–1796), the story of a weary traveler who desperately wants to go home. What becomes important is the journey itself. Here Schiller's ideas and Romanticism overlap, as he emphasized not the unrealizable goal but rather the process of education and maturation in an attempt to achieve that goal. According to the Romantics, it is the poet's responsibility to guide people to a better future.[10]

Like the Romantics, Schiller regarded boredom as plaguing modern man. To counteract this problem, he endorsed activism. His drama *William Tell* (1804) incorporates the myth of this hero with the Swiss cantons' fight for independence against the Habsburgs. In the play, it becomes obvious that traditional societies have to be challenged. Although William Tell acts alone, he represents his people and their struggle for freedom. Submerged in this drama are those general themes that tie Schiller to the Romantic authors, including the notion of free will, the ability to act on one's own volition, and human liberty.[11]

Contemporary with Goethe and Schiller and influential for Romantic aesthetics were Immanuel Kant and Johann Gottlieb Fichte. Kant, who lived and taught in Königsberg in eastern Prussia, served as a father to Romanticism even though he dismissed its adherents as fuzzy-headed thinkers. Fichte taught at the University of Jena and had direct contact with the young German Romantics resident there. What ties Immanuel Kant (1724–1804) to the Romantics is his moral philosophy and its relation to the concept of human freedom. Kant believed that things in nature, both animate and inanimate, follow rules. Man is the only creature who actually *decides* how to act. Kant also abhorred the notion that one person can control another because that would mean the second person loses his liberty. Another Kantian idea is that man creates values from within himself. Kant rejected the determinist view of some of the Enlightenment thinkers, which posits that man is simply a part of nature and acts according to preordained laws, and he supported the idea of human will and the freedom to act. Following from that, Kant suggested that man's aesthetic judgments, based on free will, allow him to recognize what is beautiful.[12]

Many Romantics adopted these ideas from Kant, but some took the notion of free will to an extreme. They suggested individuals should have complete freedom to do as they please. Kant's perspective, by contrast, limited such actions because he believed that humans have an innate sense of morality, which will prevent excessive behavior.[13] In addition, Kant's aesthetics replace individualized materialism with a generalized idealism, or in other words, the individual's particular tastes recede in favor of a general notion of what is beautiful. This allows people of different backgrounds or interests to be drawn together because they share a common notion of what is acknowledged as beautiful. This viewpoint found special resonance among many authors, including Friedrich Schiller and William Wordsworth, who feared the tendency toward what today is called the "atomization of society," where people are so distanced from one another that they have no common ground on which to relate. Kant's notion of aesthetics overrides this dilemma because the mind determines what is beautiful irrespective of the day-to-day world in which people live.[14]

Johann Gottlieb Fichte (1762–1814) arrived at the University of Jena in 1793. He impressed Goethe and became a favorite among the young German Romantics, known as the Jena Circle. For Fichte, the essence of man is action, and human knowledge allows man to survive and dominate nature.[15] Fichte emphasized the uniqueness and power of each man's mind which he called the ego or the self. He suggested that everything that is not the ego is the non-ego, which can be acted upon. In other words, the external world is the product of the human imagination.[16]

One might think that Fichte's concepts would lead to narcissism or self-obsession, but he, like Kant, restricted human freedom within the bounds of morality. His Romantic adherents interpreted the ego as "the only thing that is worthwhile ... the exfoliation of the particular self, its creative activity, its imposition of forms upon matter, its penetration of other things, its creation of values, its dedication to itself to these values."[17] The ego's search for ultimate destiny, in their opinion, was really the artist's wish to achieve perfection through a work of art.[18]

Another facet of Fichte's ideas about the need for man to act evolved in the wake of the Napoleonic wars. He believed man achieves spiritual freedom through his actions, but such activism does not always translate to physical freedom. The reality of the Napoleonic occupation of the German lands led Fichte to explore a concept associated with his fellow philosopher Johann Gottfried von Herder (1744–1803). Herder defined a community as a group of people held together by such things as shared land and language. Fichte, in turn, took this idea of community and defined it as a nation. From there, he came to be associated with the rapidly expanding German patriotism of the early nineteenth century. From 1807 to 1808, he presented a series of lectures, later published as *Addresses to the German Nation* (1808), which he hoped would enhance pride and help liberate German lands from the French yoke. (See Primary Document 4.)[19] The Romantics absorbed these views and many became associated with the growth of nationalist sentiment in the German territories and beyond.

The perspectives evident in Goethe's and Schiller's literary works and the ideas associated with Kant's and Fichte's philosophical concepts provided intellectual underpinnings for the Age of Romanticism. In addition, other contemporary forces served as stimuli. These included challenges to *ancien régime* society, reform ideas generated from Enlightenment thought, and the political and social upheaval tied to the French Revolution and the Napoleonic era. Romantic writers, artists, and musicians responded to the events and ideas around them. In a time of unprecedented change, whether caused by social, technological, or political events, it was imperative to confront these uncertainties and try to find answers.[20] The spread of a Romantic perspective occurred in identifiable steps beginning in the German-speaking lands, then moving to Great Britain, and later to France, Italy, and Russia. The Germans and the English in particular resented the cultural hegemony of the French whose stylized Classicism had dominated the eighteenth-century cultural world.

Romantic writers and artists questioned the world around them, and some even felt contemporary Western civilization teetered at the brink of disintegration. Their mission became the preservation of civilization through reexamining such timeless human values as life, liberty, hope, and joy.[21] Often, fear about the present triggers a nostalgia for the past. For many Romantics, the Middle Ages had been the best of all possible worlds with a unified Roman Catholic Church and the German states enjoying political power and prestige. Others admired the rural and local characteristics of medieval society with its absence of powerful, centralized nations and their rulers.[22]

The Romantics also looked to folk culture, such as the oral traditions of songs, tales, and legends, as a means of finding an identity for themselves and the wider community. The Germans, because of the absence of a politically united Germany, needed a means to discuss German greatness. They sought validation in myths that hearkened back to a strong and unique Germany. This practice diverged from that of the *philosophes* who had turned to the myths of Ancient

Greece and Rome, which purportedly established values that were subsequently binding on all civilization.[23] In a similar vein, French Romantic Madame de Staël (Anne Louise Germaine Necker [1766–1817]) wrote about the need for literature to reflect the spiritual essence of the place in which it was written. In *Germany* (1810) she talked about the connection of a people and its culture. Once individuals possess an idea of themselves as a unique people with their own traditions and cultural heritage, the creation of a nation-state inhabited and governed by those of the same cultural group becomes the next step.

Most Romantic writers and artists saw their duty as exploring human consciousness, revealing current problems, and describing the positive characteristics of earlier times and non-European cultures. These efforts would force individuals to rethink who and what they were, and this self-examination would lead to greater self-knowledge, wisdom, and power. The Romantics believed that when people realized the harmony of earlier times and other civilizations and saw that contemporary Western society had fallen into horrible disunity, they would address the splits in their world and rekindle connections with one another.[24]

Romantics also sought to simplify their lives, rejecting the upper-class manners and morals of eighteenth-century society. Some openly advocated an overthrow of the existing power structure in order to create a better, simpler world. Last but certainly not least, the Romantics stressed the critical role artists played in examining society. Their art was to question and challenge existing norms while causing individuals to ponder and seek the divine within themselves. This focus on the individual also manifests itself in themes ranging from the pleasures and pain of sentiment to Romantic love and suicide. In these works the individual is portrayed as the hero/heroine, the outsider, the criminal, or the person constantly searching for answers.

Since German Romanticism set the stage for what followed in other parts of Europe and the world, it is worthwhile to explore its leading figures and their ideas. The Jena Circle—that small group of individuals associated with the birth of German Romanticism—existed in a rarified intellectual atmosphere. They had indirect or direct contact with some of the greatest thinkers of their time, including Goethe, Schiller, and Kant. While these three greats openly criticized the upstart Romantics, there is no question that ideas originating with these men directly influenced Romantic thought. The most noted members of the circle included August Wilhelm von Schlegel and Karl Friedrich von Schlegel; their wives, Caroline

Michaelis Schlegel (1763–1809) and Dorothea Veit Schlegel (1763–1839); Novalis; and eventually the young Friedrich Schelling.

The Schlegel brothers, August Wilhelm (1767–1845) and Friedrich (1772–1829), defined Romanticism. While Friedrich was the original thinker, his older brother August Wilhelm was the systematic one who helped spread his brother's ideas.[25] Friedrich suggested that three things influenced the development of Romantic thinking: the French Revolution, Fichte's idea about the ego, and Goethe's novel *Wilhelm Meister's Years of Apprenticeship*.[26] Breaking with Classicism's notions of poetic rules, Friedrich suggested that modern poetry should reveal the artist's personal views. Tensions could be part of the subject matter and need not be resolved. The poet's imagination should have no limits: "there is in man a terrible unsatisfied desire to soar to infinity, a feverish longing to break through the narrow bonds of individuality."[27] The brothers rejected the Scientific Revolution's legacy of the mechanistic universe and the Enlightenment's devaluation of the importance of nature, cultural differences, the magical, and the fantastic.[28]

To expand the reach of these ideas, the brothers founded a literary journal, *The Athenaeum* (1798–1800). The Schlegels, as well as Novalis (Friedrich von Hardenberg [1772–1801]) and later Ludwig Tieck (1773–1853) among others, contributed poetry and literary criticism. Subject matter covered a gamut of themes: the nature of poetry and the poet's role in creating it; the educational demands of women; a Romantic concept of world history; the heritage of the Middle Ages; and the metric structure of verse.[29]

The youngest member of the Jena Circle, Friedrich Schelling (1775–1854) came to the university at twenty-three to teach philosophy. Before arriving, this prodigy had already published two philosophical works. He, like Fichte, talked about the ego (Schelling's term was the Absolute), a timeless entity which each person senses. Schelling ranged beyond Fichte in the discussion of nature. Schelling believed nature was not a passive but rather an active force that moved toward consciousness. The evolution from rocks, to plants, to animals reveals a developmental process toward self-consciousness. What distinguishes nature from man is that the former has no idea for what it is actually striving.[30] Man, the culmination of nature's development, also evolves, and this process parallels nature to a degree as man goes from unconscious to self-conscious in a series of steps. It is man's necessary encounters over time with other selves that lead to the emergence of the self. While Fichte suggested the self's *raison d'être* is to act, Schelling added to this concept the notion of will. It is the exercise of that will which is the essence of what it means to be human.[31]

Schelling's ideas played a critical role in the emergence of Romantic thought. Many regarded the exercise of will as a challenge to traditional values and institutions and a call to replace them with something better. More importantly, Schelling came to believe that art was the highest form of human creativity, produced by geniuses who had reached the greatest heights of self-consciousness. In the process of creating art, the artist created value that was transferred from the artist to the viewer in what becomes a quasi-religious experience.[32]

Schelling and other German writers and philosophers at the end of the eighteenth century indeed influenced the Age of Romanticism. The ideas associated with German idealist philosophy and the literary critical writings, especially those of Friedrich Schlegel, found resonance among Romantic writers, artists, and musicians across the European continent and beyond. In addition, the Romantics reacted to the Enlightenment's legacy, the growing urbanization of western Europe, and the French Revolution and the Napoleonic Wars.

Notes

1. Maurice Cranston, *The Romantic Movement* (Cambridge, MA: Blackwell, 1994), 11–13.

2. Ibid., 14.

3. Thomas McFarland, *Romanticism and the Heritage of Rousseau* (Oxford: Clarendon Press, 1995), 51–52.

4. Cranston, *The Romantic Movement*, 48–49, 51.

5. Aidan Day, *Romanticism* (New York: Routledge, 1996), 49–50; Anne K. Mellor, *Romanticism and Gender* (New York: Routledge, 1993), 108.

6. Herbert Frenzel and Elizabeth Frenzel, *Daten deutscher Dichtung Chronologischer Abriß der deutschen Literaturgeschichte, Band I*, 3rd ed. (Cologne: DTW, 1998), 201–230.

7. Ibid., 203–204. To capitalize on the interest in the past, Scotsman James Macpherson published *Fragments of Ancient Poetry, collected in the Highlands of Scotland*, in 1760. The poems and songs allegedly originated with an ancient bard named Ossian. It was eventually proved that Macpherson had forged the documents.

8. Ibid., 204–206.

9. Cranston, *The Romantic Movement*, 46–47; Isaiah Berlin, *The Roots of Romanticism* (Princeton, NJ: Princeton University Press, 1999), 111.

10. M. H. Abrams, *Natural Supernaturalism: Tradition and Revolution in Romantic Literature* (New York: W. W. Norton, 1971), 211–213, 215–216, 350.

11. Gerald Gillespie, "Agents and Agency in the History of Romantic Literature," in *The People's Voice: Essays on European Romanticism*, ed.

Andrea Ciccarelli et al. (Melbourne: Monash University, 1999), 48; Berlin, *Roots of Romanticism*, 78.

12. Berlin, *Roots of Romanticism*, 68–75.

13. Paul Roubiczek, "Some Aspects of German Philosophy in the Romantic Period," in *The Romantic Period in Germany*, ed. Siegbert Prawer (New York: Schocken Books, 1970), 306–308.

14. David Simpson, "Transcendental Philosophy and Romantic Criticism," in *The Cambridge History of Literary Criticism, Vol. 5, Romanticism*, ed. Marshall Brown (New York: Cambridge University Press, 2000), 87–88.

15. Berlin, *Roots of Romanticism*, 88.

16. Cranston, *The Romantic Movement*, 28–29; Robert Richards, *The Romantic Conception of Life: Science and Philosophy in the Age of Goethe* (Chicago: University of Chicago Press, 2002), 79.

17. Berlin, *Roots of Romanticism*, 95.

18. Richards, *The Romantic Conception of Life*, 83.

19. Berlin, *Roots of Romanticism*, 90–91.

20. Abrams, *Natural Supernaturalism*, 292–293.

21. Ibid., 431.

22. Herbert Schenk, *The Mind of the European Romantics* (Garden City, NY: Doubleday, 1969), 32–38.

23. Berlin, *Roots of Romanticism*, 121–122.

24. Abrams, *Natural Supernaturalism*, 255–256.

25. Morse Peckham, *The Birth of Romanticism, 1790–1815* (Greenwood, FL: Penkeville Publishing Co., 1986), 130.

26. Three different sources mentioned these concepts, but one attributed the notion to August Wilhelm (Berlin, *Roots of Romanticism*, 93), whereas two other sources attributed the list to Friedrich, which seems more likely. Those sources were Frenzel, *Daten deutscher Dichtung*, 296, and Siegbert Prawer, "Introduction," in *The Romantic Period in Germany*, 11.

27. Richards, *The Romantic Conception of Life*, 21; Friedrich Schlegel as quoted in Berlin, *Roots of Romanticism*, 15.

28. Max Blechman, "The Revolutionary Dream of Early German Romanticism," in *Revolutionary Romanticism* (San Francisco: City Lights Books, 1999), 12.

29. Oscar Walzel, *German Romanticism* (New York: Capricorn Books, 1966), 45, 83, 94–95, 107–108, 132.

30. Berlin, *Roots of Romanticism*, 98–99.

31. Peckham, *The Birth of Romanticism*, 108–110. Schelling expressed his views about the will in his book *The System of Transcendental Idealism*.

32. Ibid., 110–112.

CHAPTER 2

"MINUTES OF ACTIVE SENSITIVITY": ROMANTIC POETRY

For poets there "exist minutes of active sensitivity: people with real talent have experienced them; artists, musicians and, most of all, poets must be quick to grasp them for they are rare, fleeting...." Moreover, poetry has been called "that heavenly flame, which more or less, is an organic part of the human soul (that combination of imagination, sensitivity and reverie)...."[1] This perspective venerates poets, their creative imagination, and their poetry, and justifies their special status in society. Many Romantic poets accepted this fate and sought inspiration that would ignite their creative spark. This search led some to intense religiosity, misguided love affairs, or substance abuse, and so on. The despair at not finding proper inspiration led some Romantic poets to commit suicide. Others recounted moments of youthful creativity in an effort to regain needed momentum in their later years.

From about 1790 identifiably Romantic poetry appeared in print, but theoretical discussions defining it emerged at the end of that decade. Some general characteristics connect European Romantic poetry: (1) it followed no prescribed rules; (2) it reflected the national environment in which it was created; and, (3) it used rich language to describe great history, heroes, landscapes, and the like.[2] Also, many Romantic poems explored the theme of the poet as a prophet whose imaginative powers and creative efforts helped explain the mysteries of the world to ordinary people.

The Germans

Novalis [Friedrich von Hardenberg], a mining engineer, reached beyond his scientific background to search nature for metaphysical meaning. For him the Enlightenment's attempts to reconcile reason and nature had failed. Moreover, the French Revolution had destroyed the *ancien régime* but had not provided a blueprint for the future. He did not advocate political or social revolution, rather he wanted writers to create a new spiritual culture. Poetry was the bond that tied man to nature, and poets should serve as agents to connect man and the universe.[3]

Novalis's contribution to Romantic poetry, his prose poem, *"Hymnen an die Nacht"* ("Hymns to the Night" [1802]), explores his intense feelings of loss after his fiancée's death. The first four hymns discuss loneliness, the death wish, and the desire to be reunited with his beloved after death. Novalis turned traditional images upside down, portraying night and darkness, not day and light, as positive. For him, night was holy, the mother of the world and true existence, because it allowed man total freedom. The last two hymns identify Novalis's religion of the night with Christianity and, more particularly, Jesus Christ as the victor over death. His reversal of images reveals Novalis's link to the Romantic notion that the poet must direct mankind to an awareness of new cultural values.[4]

Johann Christian Friedrich Hölderlin (1770–1843), one of Germany's greatest lyric poets, modeled his poems after Classical themes, but he must be considered a Romantic because of his fascination with the divine, mysterious, and natural. He often wrote about the Greek gods, but, in Romantic fashion, knowledge of them came through the poet's imagination rather than divine inspiration.[5] His elegy, *"Brot und Wein"* ["Bread and Wine" (1801)], has three parts: (1) a general discussion of night; (2) the day, associated with Ancient Greece and the revelation of the Olympian gods; and, (3) the night of current Western civilization. From his perspective the greatest highlight of human history occurred when the Greek gods revealed themselves. By contrast, modern man is currently in darkness waiting for a new event that will provide religious insight. When that occurs, modern man will find happiness, but until then the poet must explain man's current dilemma.[6]

The English Romantics

William Blake (1757–1827), although not appreciated in his time, embodies the essence of Romanticism. As with many of his contemporaries, Blake welcomed the French Revolution because he believed society had to undergo conflict in order to appreciate the contrast between authority and liberty or, in his terms, between experience and innocence. In 1789 and 1794 Blake's poetry volumes, *Songs of Innocence* and *Songs of Experience*, appeared. Poems from the earlier collection praise childhood as the perfect, unspoiled age and predict the dawning of a new era when powerful political and religious institutions will be overthrown. These poems reveal Blake's views on nature and humanity, which parallel those of Rousseau; Blake, however, did have more faith in the goodness of man, perhaps because he believed the Christian message of Jesus the Redeemer. In *Songs of Experience*, published after the Terror of the French Revolution, Blake's poems explore political, social, religious, and aesthetic topics and the power of the imagination. More importantly, they point to the poet as a disseminator of critical ideas that transform the world. (See Primary Document 5.)[7]

Blake viewed his world as fractured on a physical level because of the spread of industrial production and its effects on society. In fact, Blake coined the term "dark satanic mills" in reference to those events. On a spiritual level, Blake believed man possessed inborn ideas, especially notions about morality and beauty. Although humans have a built-in conscience, or "voice of God," it is not always easy to do the right thing.[8] Blake suggested that the imagination, man's most creative faculty, makes us human and must bring mankind back to his previous innocence. The best guides are the artists who, because of their aesthetic imagination, can perceive an eternal, unchanging world, while ordinary people only see the everyday world, limited by the rules of time and space. The artists' creations serve as the guides that provide access to Blake's ideal world: a free community of people, where all can realize their full potential.[9]

Blake's views not only appeared in his poems, but also in his engravings and paintings. They depict simple, stylized figures, with drawing more important than color. The drama that appears in his works is unique to Blake but nevertheless reveals the influence of contemporaries such as his friend Henry Fuseli (1741–1825), whose dramatic nudes and fantasies encouraged Blake to explore his feelings through what appear to be distortions on canvas.

Blake's slightly younger contemporaries, Samuel Taylor Coleridge (1772–1834) and William Wordsworth (1770–1850), are synonymous with the Age of Romanticism. Coleridge, a philosopher and poet, met William Wordsworth in 1795 when both men were dealing with disillusionment associated with the French Revolution. Between

1797 and 1798, Coleridge wrote several poems, including "The Rime of the Ancient Mariner" and "Kubla Khan," both of which appeared in *Lyrical Ballads* (1798), the volume which signaled the birth of Romanticism in Britain. "The Rime of the Ancient Mariner" describes a mariner whose ship and crew encounter a storm at sea. An albatross appears, signaling their survival, and becomes the ship's good luck symbol. After the mariner kills the albatross, the cursed ship is becalmed, and slowly two hundred crewmen die, immortalized in the words: "Water, water, every where,/ And all the boards did shrink;/ Water, water, every where,/ Nor any drop to drink." The wretched mariner survives and experiences a rebirth. He eventually returns home, and as penance he has to constantly travel and teach others to love all God's creatures.

Interpretations of the poem vary: one view suggests it describes an individual's relationship to his culture. In shooting the albatross, the mariner committed a crime against his community. Another view suggests a religious message because Coleridge added commentary to a later version which explains the mariner's fate as sin, repentance, and redemption. Yet a third perspective explores a psychological view: the mariner experiences isolation and alienation. He eventually realizes nature is always there, connecting him to the wider universe, even when he does not sense it.[10]

Coleridge's other masterpiece, "Kubla Khan," has been discussed from various perspectives, too. Coleridge tells the tale of exotic Xanadu in all its fertile lushness. In one view, he describes the artist's vision; it is a world of contradictions, both peaceful and violent. The damsel represents the poet's sensibility, and if she is able to reclaim her song, the poet will reclaim his vision. But this cannot happen because the vision is only a dream. Another, darker, view suggests the beautiful garden of the Khan (which represents culture) will not rise above the terrors associated with it: ice, "measureless" caverns, and the "sunless sea." Others suggest that the poem reveals the opium-induced images Coleridge experienced while writing it.[11]

Coleridge's views about the imagination have a religious association because to him imagination was God's gift to humans, which allows them to perceive and appreciate creation. Only artists had what Coleridge called poetic imagination, which distinguishes them from everyone else. This gift gave artists, especially poets, a special mission to bring mankind back to unity which had been lost due to contemporary stresses that had drawn man away from his essential nature and isolated him from others and himself. These ideas are explored in his *Biographia Literaria* (*Literary Biography* [1817]).[12]

Coleridge's observations about the poet's special calling manifest themselves in the life of William Wordsworth. He can be credited with creating a new poetic tradition, which incorporated not only original themes but also new language. Rejecting the formal, stylized poetry of the early eighteenth century, Wordsworth believed the language of poems should be like that spoken by ordinary people. (See Primary Document 6.)[13] He included such poems in *Lyrical Ballads*, published anonymously in 1798. The critics regarded them as experiments, but that is exactly what Wordsworth intended, and he justified what he had done in the "Preface" to the editions of *Lyrical Ballads*, which appeared in 1800 and 1802.

"Lines Composed A Few Miles Above Tintern Abbey" (1798) is Wordsworth's longest poem in *Lyrical Ballads*. In it, he recounts a walk that he and his sister Dorothy took along the river Wye in 1798. It also reflects on a visit there five years earlier. Then he had sought beauty in the river valley, but in the intervening time, his world has fallen apart. In the poem, he asks nature to help answer questions that will solve his spiritual crisis.[14]

Wordsworth's epic, *The Prelude*, "the most sustained exploration of the self in English Romantic literature," was completed in 1805, but not published until after his death.[15] While it recounts Wordsworth's personal history, what is critical is how the events he experienced shaped his mind. It first describes Wordsworth's childhood and youth and how his intense love of nature led him to equivalent feelings about humanity. Then it explains his favorable response to the revolutionary events in France because of his love of humanity and then how the revolution's excesses crushed his enthusiasm. The narrative reveals how he came to terms with this disappointment and how it affected his creative abilities. The conclusion returns to nature and recounts how Wordsworth saw himself as a means to instruct others to value their minds and to exercise them in the search for God.[16] This poem embodies Romantic themes, since not only is the poet the primary subject, but the concept of genius is delineated.[17]

The Prelude also recounts Wordsworth's relationship to nature which can implant itself on the human spirit and cause feelings of fear and beauty. Wordsworth, following Edmund Burke's concepts, described "the sublime" as vast, wild, awful, painful, and terrible but also capable of evoking admiration. In contrast, "the beautiful" referred to order, tranquility, pleasure, and, most importantly, love.[18] *The Prelude* also explores the notion of "self" insofar as Wordsworth discusses the self in its historical context through the story of his life and the events surrounding the French Revolution. Wordsworth does not highlight activities in the everyday world but rather in the world of the mind. By abandoning the world outside for that of the mind, a person experiences genuine freedom of the inner self through the growth of consciousness.[19]

Throughout his works, but especially in an essay in *Poems* (1815), Wordsworth dealt with the role of the poet in society. To be original, the poet must explore subject matter that has universal rather than transitory themes. Wordsworth suggests that poets, with their special insights about the world, can play the role of poet-prophet.[20] Percy Bysshe Shelley (1792–1822) agreed with William Wordsworth's notion of the poet's importance to society when he referred to his fellow poets as "the authors to others of the highest wisdom, pleasure, virtue and glory."[21]

Shelley felt the poet should be engaged in commentary about and involvement in the real world. He became disappointed with Wordsworth and Coleridge who appeared to have abandoned political idealism and activism. This feeling led him to William Godwin's (1756–1836) *An Enquiry Concerning Political Justice* (1793), which warns against political power and the tendency for governments to force people to conform. Godwin's book became Shelley's guide and provided him with an idealism about social and political change that appears in his first major poem, *Queen Mab* (1813). In it, he criticizes governments, religion, and other institutions. Shelley's notes about the poem reflect his thoughts on how natural equality between people was preferable to the current society with its extremes of rich and poor, and how a better world could be created.[22]

Shelley's greatest poem, *Prometheus Unbound* (1820), loosely relates to the Ancient Greek myth of Prometheus who disobeyed Zeus and provided mankind with fire. For punishment, Zeus chained Prometheus to a rock where an eagle devoured his liver; each night it regenerated, and the next day the eagle returned. Shelley's Prometheus is incomplete because of his separation from his love, Asia, after an angry Jupiter (the Roman god equivalent to Zeus) has bound him to a rock. To reach Prometheus, Asia must travel to the underworld where she confronts a demon to ask, "What causes evil?" He claims he does not know. Asia journeys on and eventually learns that love is the only way to overcome the dilemma. After the lovers reunite, they need to cultivate their love for that will keep them whole. Interpretations vary as to whether Shelley's primary concern is the individual human mind, or the body and soul, or wider society in general. Regardless, good triumphs over evil in this poem.[23]

Another Romantic theme found in Shelley's poetry examines the poet and his role in society. This theme is eloquently explored in "Adonais" (1821), Shelley's lament over John Keats. Shelley truly

regrets Keats's death, but on a broader scale, Shelley sees himself—
the poet—as a martyr, recognizing that the world kills poets because
it does not truly understand them. Only after death are the great
poets really appreciated.[24] Shelley drowned in a boating accident at
age thirty with so many unanswered questions surrounding him and
his potential. His fellow Romantic, George Gordon, Lord Byron
(1788–1824), also died young but not before his lifestyle and literary
legacy became the center of attention for European high society.

In the wake of his grand tour, Byron published the first two
parts of *Childe Harold's Pilgrimage* (1812), which recounts a complex
young man's European travels; whether or not it can be considered
an autobiographical work is still debated. Regardless, it describes distant exotic places as friendly, whereas his native land seems overcome by sadness. The hero's lost vision, a hallmark of Romantic
poetry, pervades the poem. When the third canto, in which Byron
explores his fascination with Napoleon, appeared later, his English
critics accused him of being unpatriotic.[25] Despite this, Byron
became more popular than any other English author of his time.

Between 1818 and 1822 the different parts of *Don Juan*
appeared. Critics debate whether this is a great satire or a marvelous
epic; nevertheless, this lengthy poem reveals Byron's comic side. The
adventures of hapless Don Juan unfold in two thousand stanzas, but
as they do, the story reveals opinions about contemporary moral values and the nature of political institutions.[26] Serious philosophical
questions about the nature of man and his existence are posed as
Don Juan journeys on. Here, another Romantic theme appears: life
as one long journey.

Byron's greatest literary legacy is his heroes who, even though
disreputable figures, experience the throes of love. Being in love
causes them to transcend their undesirable characteristics and rise
above society's norms. His heroes have already been formed by previous life experiences, and they often confront a world they reject or
whose values they scorn. The Byronic hero's experiences reveal the
prominent themes found in his poetry: loss, alienation, isolation, abandonment, disenchantment, and the sense of failure of one's culture.[27]

Byron kept in touch with other British expatriates then living
abroad, including Shelley. The two poets discussed creating a new
literary journal around 1820, and Shelley invited John Keats (1795–
1821), whom he had met in London in 1816, to visit Italy. Keats had
published a small book of poetry in 1817, and despite little recogni-
tion, he was subsequently asked to write a long poem based on the
Greek myth of Endymion, the mortal loved by the moon goddess. In
the myth, she does not want her lover to die, so Zeus gives him

eternal sleep. In Keats's *Endymion*, the hero, a shepherd king, falls in love with Cynthia, an enchanting beauty he meets in a dream. Whenever he is about to gain Cynthia, he loses her. The object of the hero's quest is never attained. For Keats, this state reflects modern life and the destiny of the poet—to recount that no vision can ever be permanently fixed or attained.[28]

Hostile reviews of *Endymion* appeared in various literary magazines in 1818. To disprove his critics, Keats began his most productive artistic period in the spring of 1819 in which he wrote several odes which explore themes including the nature of youth, beauty, and life. One of the best known, "Ode on a Grecian Urn," describes scenes captured forever on an urn: the lovers about to kiss, the beautiful trees, the priest with a sacrificial animal, and a village.[29] Throughout 1819 and into the next year, Keats worked on his poem *Hyperion*, which described the Roman god Saturn's fall from divinity and the evils he endured. Keats then reworked the poem, giving it a more personal direction, and renamed it *The Fall of Hyperion* (1820). Here, he returned to established Romantic themes: that "human growth and creativity can only occur if there is suffering and loss."[30]

In addition to his beautiful poetry, Keats often wrote letters to friends and family. Those written to his brothers reveal his appreciation of nature and curiosity about new things. (See Primary Document 7.) Keats believed in the special mission of the poet: to use his gift of vision to describe a better, moral world. He was initially inspired by nature but then turned to more spiritual things such as notions of beauty and truth for motivation.[31]

One of the ways contemporary critics attacked Keats was to portray him as "feminine." Not only was he a diminutive man, but his lack of a university education also placed him among those female authors trying to make their marks as poets.[32] Such attacks reflected a trend evident at this time: more women were publishing poetry. Even though many believed that *only* men could write great poetry, in Britain between 1770 and 1830, women dominated the literary market and many wrote poetry.[33]

British women poets have enjoyed a renaissance, as recent scholarship has turned to investigating their lives and works. Even Dorothy Wordsworth (1771–1855), whose journals initially served as a means to study her brother and Coleridge, has been recognized in her own right.[34] While Anna Lætitia Barbauld (1743–1825), Mary Robinson (1758–1800), Jane Taylor (1783–1824), and Letitia Elizabeth Landon (1802–1838), among others, might not be known by anyone other than students of British literature, they contributed to Romanticism's literary legacy. Women poets chose shorter forms such as the ballad and the sonnet to express their ideas. These writers explored personal feelings, their poems often taking the form of a conversation between the writer and the reader.[35]

Felicia Browne Hemans (1793–1835) was England's best-selling poet, sandwiched between Lord Byron and Alfred, Lord Tennyson (1809–1892) chronologically. Her poetry appeared in popular journals that appealed to the middle-class reading audience. Influenced by Byron, she wrote her epic *The Forest Sanctuary* (1825), which explores the relationship between family allegiance and the power of the state. Set in sixteenth-century Spain, a family confronts the Spanish Inquisition and its search for heretics. Not willing to risk possible execution, a father decides to take his family to the New World, but his wife dies en route. Once in America, he longs for home, but he also recognizes that he and his son can now enjoy true freedom.[36]

Hemans's poetry stands out in its praise of the finer feelings, especially as they relate to family life and women's self-sacrifice. But an inherent contradiction resides with Hemans, too, because, while she praises woman in her domestic role, Hemans herself existed in the wider world, competing with men and other women to get published. She was certainly aware of the contradiction and discussed it in "The Last Song of Sappho" (1839). (See Primary Document 8.)[37]

An Italian Example

One characteristic of Romanticism as it developed on the European continent was its connection to emerging nationalism, especially in Italy. A conglomeration of states, Italy had suffered under Napoleonic and later Austrian domination. Most writers became involved in public affairs, which gave their works political motifs, especially the theme of promoting freedom.[38]

An Italian Romantic, mainly known for his poetry and deeply involved with his country's struggles, was Ugo Foscolo (1778–1827). His tragedy *Tieste* brought him literary fame in 1797, and, as with most of his works, it shows both Classical and Romantic influences. Politically, he had endorsed Napoleon as a liberator of Italy. Expecting that French troops would remove the stagnant oligarchy from his native Venice, Foscolo wrote an ode to the general. Foscolo soon became disillusioned, especially after Napoleon signed a treaty with the Austrians, giving them control of Venice. Dealing with that shock, Foscolo wrote the novel, *The Last Letters of Jacopo Ortis* (1802), which describes a young man who eventually commits suicide because of the conflict between his lady love and service to his country. As a literary work, *Jacopo Ortis* has been compared to Goethe's *The Sorrows of Young Werther* and Rousseau's *Julie, or The New Eloise*. But unlike those novels, Foscolo's exhibits a greater national connection because of his use of Italian history and society as the background.[39]

Foscolo's other major literary work, "Of the Sepulchers" (1807), is a 295-line poem that attacks Napoleon's law forbidding inscriptions on tombs. Foscolo disagreed with this prohibition and suggested that prominent Italians' tombs should serve as sites to inspire people about their heritage. He believed the emulation of Italy's long-dead heroes will help his contemporaries through their times of trouble and overcome their skepticism about an uncertain future. Foscolo's poem serves as a rallying cry for Italian patriotism and revisits the Romantic notion that poets should be involved in the contemporary world.

The Russians

Two individuals served as important facilitators of Russian Romanticism: Nikolai Karamzin (1766–1826) and Vasily Zhukovsky (1783–1852). Karamzin, a recognized historian, played a critical role because of his challenge to accepted literary standards. He did not want to follow the dictates of classical Russian prose, which he regarded as too heavily laden with medieval Church-Slavonic, the Russian Orthodox Church's official language. His initial effort at writing Russian in a lighter style was *Letters of a Russian Traveler, 1789–1790* (1792) in which the Russian he used was influenced by French conversational style. He wrote poems, such as "Spring Song of a Melancholic" (1788) and "Autumn" (1789), with a sentimental lilt, and if they are not considered Romantic themselves, they certainly foreshadow the movement. The former expresses the contradiction within the poet, the joy at the onset of spring and his personal anguish with the remnants of winter in his soul. "Autumn" explores a contradictory theme, a favorite Romantic practice: the onset of winter reminds one of both human mortality and nature's immortality.[40]

Vasily Zhukovsky contributed to Russian Romanticism in three ways. First, he translated European works into Russian, including those of Sir Walter Scott and Lord Byron. Second, Zhukovsky wrote poetry using Karamzin's more lyrical Russian in which Zhukovsky explored feelings such as love and friendship. He, like the German Romantics, set many poems against the backdrop of fog and deepest night. Zhukovsky believed in the poet's unique mission to use his inspiration, a gift from God, to guide the average person. His poems are credited with having a rhythmic quality; for example, in "The Sea, an Elegy" (1822), one can sense the waves' motion.[41]

Zhukovsky's third contribution to Russian Romanticism was to inspire Aleksandr Sergeyevich Pushkin (1799–1837), arguably Russia's greatest poet. Pushkin's poem *Ruslan and Ludmila* (1820) was criticized by the literary establishment because its content and style violated Classical rules. The hero Ruslan, modeled after the heroes of traditional Russian folk epics, experiences numerous adventures during his quest to rescue his bride Ludmila. Building upon Karamzin's legacy, Pushkin wrote in the vernacular and, like Wordsworth, felt it was important to use everyday language in his poems.[42]

Pushkin's works share many themes common to other Romantics. Like Byron, Pushkin's poetry is replete with heroes, and his ballads are often set in exotic locales. A popular Romantic theme, the clash between civilized man and the noble savage, appears in "The Gypsies" (1824). It is a tale told mostly through dreams in which a young gypsy, Zemfira, discovers a man, Aleko, wandering on the steppe. She brings him back to her camp, and he falls in love with her. But like her namesake, "the wind," she refuses to be controlled. When she rejects his demands and turns to another lover, Aleko kills them both.[43]

Pushkin's anguish over the failed Decembrist Uprising in 1825 (a revolt against Tsar Nicholas I [ruled 1825–1855]) caused him to conclude that if reform was to come to Russia it had to be directed by the tsar. He then immersed himself in studying Peter the Great (ruled 1689–1725) who opened Russia to the West and built St. Petersburg. Pushkin's resulting masterpiece, "The Bronze Horseman" (1837), focuses on an ordinary man, Yevgeny, whose sweetheart is drowned in the raging waters of the Neva River. Driven mad by the event, he rushes around the flooded city, eventually coming to rest near a bronze equestrian statue of Peter the Great. When Yevgeny threatens the tsar because it is his fault the city was constructed on a floodplain, the statue comes to life and chases the poor man through the city's streets. Three important Russian Romantic literary themes emerge: (1) the plight of the little man in the face of social superiors; (2) St. Petersburg as a city where mysterious events occur; and (3) the mixed historical reputation of Peter the Great.[44]

Pushkin's slightly younger fellow poet and admirer, Mikhail Yurievich Lermontov (1814–1841), developed his Romantic literary tendencies after he was exposed to Byron's poetry. Although he began writing poetry at thirteen, his great poems came about during the last five years of his life. Like many Romantics, he explored such themes as loneliness, personal liberty, the hero's plight, and, of course, the poet in society. Lermontov believed that the poet's inherent loneliness is due to the fact that society basically misunderstands such individuals.

Lermontov gained fame through his elegy "Death of a Poet" (1837). In it, he blames aristocratic society, and by implication the tsar, for Pushkin's death. (A court intrigue and the probable infidelity of his wife led Pushkin to challenge her lover to a duel in which the poet died.) When the tsar became aware of the poem, he banished Lermontov from the capital. He returned to St. Petersburg within a year, where he emerged as a prominent literary figure, being hailed as Pushkin's successor. Lermontov took inspiration from Russia's folktales and rich history. This is evident in "A Song about Tsar Ivan Vasilyevich, His Young Bodyguard and the Valiant Merchant Kalashnikov" (1837). Set during the reign of Ivan the Terrible (ruled 1530–1584), it describes the treachery of one of the tsar's bodyguards, which leads the beloved merchant Kalashnikov to seek retribution because of the dishonor brought upon his family. The poem's cadence is reminiscent of a traditional folk song. Despite its sixteenth-century setting, its themes elicit emotions that transcend the ages.[45]

Another noted Russian Romantic poet is Fyodor Ivanovich Tyutchev (1803–1873), who encountered German Romantic poetry while a student at Moscow University. After brief study in St. Petersburg at the Collegium of Foreign Affairs, he received a diplomatic posting to Munich. Coincident with his residence abroad, Tyutchev began to write lyric poetry. "Silentium," written in 1833, explores a theme common to Romantic verse: the gulf between the poet and the people. Since they really cannot fathom what he is trying to tell them, they want him to be silent![46]

Like Novalis, Tyutchev addressed the theme of night. During the night man confronts himself for what he really is, and there is no escaping that truth. In the second stanza of "Day and Night" (1839), he says: "And now the chasm greets our sight/With its dark terrors; once we've seen it,/There is no obstacle between it/And us— that's why we fear the night!"[47] Tyutchev's choice of language, favoring such words as "mystery" and "chaos," also reveals the German writer's influence.[48]

While Russian poetry mirrored that found among the German and English Romantics—subjects such as nature, love, and the critical role of the artist in society—the theme of political exile can be found in their works. In fact, like the Italians, Russian poets integrated current political themes into their works. This strong connection between poetry and politics led critics to disdain women poets whose themes tended to be apolitical. Nevertheless, Russian women wrote poetry, and the most noted was Karolina Pavlova (1807–1893). Her father, a German, married a Russian, and Karolina grew up in a trilingual household. She translated poetry from German and French into Russian, and her first poetry volume appeared in German. She tried to overcome her ambiguous status by leaning toward Slavophilism, which rejected Western influence in Russia and sought out authentic Russia in its peasant past. She wrote "A Conversation in the Kremlin" (1854), which occurs among a Frenchman, an Englishman, and a Russian who becomes the spokesman for Russia's great historical triumphs.[49]

Pavlova also addressed the belief that women could not write superior poetry. Her "Three Souls" (1845) confronts this theme, since the souls are three women poets. Each suffers tragically: one loses her poetic gift because she is drawn into high society; one becomes a hopeless dreamer and dies young; and the last suffers the loss of her poetic voice because she can never realize her dream. Pavlova's later poems reflect her challenge to the prevailing stereotypes. "Life calls us" (1846) is regarded as a major work that illustrates her commitment. In it, she reflects on the past and her friends and mentors of those years, especially Pushkin and Lermontov. But rather than dwell on loss and separation from those individuals, Pavlova discusses them as part of a network that contributed to her development as a poet.[50]

Ranging from England in the West across the European continent to Russia, Romantic poets shared a similar view. They regarded themselves as the means by which, because of their poetic imagination, life's important messages could be captured and conveyed to ordinary people through poetry. Their art enriched everyone's lives, even though many poets felt that wider society misunderstood, if not outright rejected, them.

Notes

1. K. N. Batyushkov, "A Word About the Poet and Poetry," in *The Ardis Anthology of Russian Romanticism*, ed. Christine Rydel (Ann Arbor, MI: Ardis, 1984), 381.

2. From Russian journalist Orest Samov's essay "On Romantic Poetry" (1823) as mentioned in John Mersereau Jr., "Yes Virginia, There Was a Russian Romantic Movement," in *The Ardis Anthology of Russian Romanticism*, 514.

3. Morse Peckham, *The Birth of Romanticism, 1790–1815* (Greenwood, FL: Penkeville Publishing Co., 1986), 135, 139–142; Nicholas Riasonovsky, *The Emergence of Romanticism* (New York: Oxford University Press, 1992), 51.

4. Gerald Gillespie, "Agents and Agency in the History of Romantic Literature," in *The People's Voice: Essays on European Romanticism*, ed. Andrea Ciccarelli et al. (Melbourne: Monash University, 1999), 50–51; Peckham, *The Birth of Romanticism*, 140–141.

5. Peckham, *The Birth of Romanticism*, 160–161.

6. Richard Unger, *Hölderlin's Major Poetry: The Dialectics of Unity* (Bloomington: Indiana University Press, 1975), 69–80, 82–83.

7. Peter Marshall, "William Blake: Revolutionary Romantic," in *Revolutionary Romanticism*, ed. Max Blechman (San Francisco: City Lights Press, 1999), 57; Maurice Cranston, *The Romantic Movement* (Cambridge, MA: Blackwell, 1994), 54–55; David Morse, *Romanticism: A Structural Analysis* (Totowa, NJ: Barnes and Noble, 1982), 234–235.

8. Marshall, "William Blake," 42–48.

9. M. H. Abrams, *Natural Supernaturalism: Tradition and Revolution in Romantic Literature* (New York: W. W. Norton, 1971), 261; Marshall, "William Blake," 42–43, 46, 62.

10. Peckham, *The Birth of Romanticism*, 126; Abrams, *Natural Supernaturalism*, 272–273; Morse, *Romanticism*, 261.

11. Morse, *Romanticism*, 260–261; Peckham, *The Birth of Romanticism*, 129; Althea Hayter, *Opium and the Romantic Imagination* (Los Angeles: University of California Press, 1968), 215–216.

12. Cranston, *The Romantic Movement*, 61; Morse, *Romanticism*, 259; Abrams, *Natural Supernaturalism*, 379.

13. Peckham, *The Birth of Romanticism*, 116–117; Maurice Hindle, "Revolting Language: British Romantics in an Age of Revolution," in *Revolutionary Romantics*, 69–70.

14. Abrams, *Natural Supernaturalism*, 92; Peckham, *The Birth of Romanticism*, 119.

15. Cranston, *The Romantic Movement*, 61.

16. Philip Connell, *Romanticism, Economics and the "Question of Culture"* (New York: Oxford University Press, 2001), 42; Peckham, *The Birth of Romanticism*, 221–222; William Wordsworth, *The Prelude, 1799, 1805, 1850*, ed. Jonathan Wordsworth et al. (New York: W. W. Norton, 1979), 482, n. 9.

17. Morse, *Romanticism*, 256.

18. Abrams, *Natural Supernaturalism*, 98; Peckham, *The Birth of Romanticism*, 223.

19. Thomas McFarland, *Romanticism and the Heritage of Rousseau* (Oxford: Clarendon Press, 1995), 41; Anne K. Mellor, *Romanticism and Gender* (New York: Routledge, 1993), 145, 147.

20. Abrams, *Natural Supernaturalism*, 391–397, 406–407, 430.

21. As quoted in Abrams, *Natural Supernaturalism*, 428.

22. Hindle, "Revolting Language," 73; Cranston, *The Romantic Movement*, 64–65; Aidan Day, *Romanticism* (New York: Routledge, 1996), 158–162.

23. Abrams, *Natural Supernaturalism*, 299–305.

24. Morse, *Romanticism*, 282.

25. Cranston, *The Romantic Movement*, 72; John D. Jump, "Byron: The Historical Context," in *Byron's Poetry*, ed. Frank D. McConnell (New York: W. W. Norton, 1978), 357; Morse, *Romanticism*, 288.

26. Day, *Romanticism*, 168–169.

27. Morse, *Romanticism*, 284–289; Peckham, *The Birth of Romanticism*, 333–334.

28. Morse, *Romanticism*, 264–265.

29. Ibid., 263.

30. Abrams, *Natural Supernaturalism*, 128.

31. Cranston, *The Romantic Movement*, 67–68.

32. Mellor, *Romanticism and Gender*, 172.

33. Anne K. Mellor, "Feminism," in *Romanticism: An Oxford Guide*, ed. Nicholas Roe (New York: Oxford University Press, 2005), 182. Also, see *Romantics: Women Poets of the Romantic Period, 1770–1830*, 12 vols., ed. Caroline Franklin (New York: Routledge, 1996).

34. Susan M. Levin, *Dorothy Wordsworth and Romanticism* (New Brunswick, NJ: Rutgers University Press, 1987), reproduces all of Dorothy's known poetry.

35. Mellor, "Feminism," 191.

36. Chad Edgar, "Felicia Hemans and the Shifting Field of Romanticism," in *Felicia Hemans: Re-imagining Poetry in the Nineteenth Century*, ed. Nanora Sweet and Julie Melnyk (New York: Palgrave, 2001), 124–125.

37. Stuart Curran, "Women Readers, Women Writers," in *The Cambridge Companion to British Romanticism* (New York: Cambridge University Press, 1993), 190–191; Marlon B. Ross, *The Contours of Masculine Desire* (New York: Oxford University Press, 1989), 289–290, 299.

38. Cranston, *The Romantic Movement*, 104.

39. Ibid., 99; Peckham, *The Birth of Romanticism*, 174–181.

40. Mersereau, "Yes Virginia," 512, 514; Christine Rydel, "Lyric Poetry: Introduction," in *The Ardis Anthology of Russian Romanticism*, 21–22.

41. Mersereau, "Yes Virginia," 512; Rydel, "Lyric Poetry: Introduction," 22–24.

42. Rydel, "Lyric Poetry: Introduction," 27.

43. Christine Rydel, "Ballads and Verse Narratives: Introduction," in *The Ardis Anthology of Russian Romanticism*, 103.

44. Ibid., 107.

45. Ibid., 102.

46. Rydel, "Lyric Poetry: Introduction," 44.

47. The entire poem is found in *The Ardis Anthology of Russian Romanticism*, 93.

48. Rydel, "Lyric Poetry: Introduction," 45.

49. Catriona Kelly, *A History of Russian Women's Writing, 1820–1992* (New York: Oxford University Press, 1994), 35–36, 39–41, 93–95, 112.

50. Ibid., 98–99.

CHAPTER 3

ROMANTIC PROSE AND DRAMA

Despite poetry's predominance as *the* exalted Romantic genre, other forms became part of the literary canon, including the fairy tale, the novella, the novel, and the drama. Whereas poets could use their special gifts and imaginations to interpret the Infinite for mere mortals in verse, prose authors had to resort to incorporating magic or the supernatural in what appeared to be a realistic story and to creating situations that unleashed fear or uncertainty in order to reach the sublime.

The Genres

"Once upon a time, in a land far away, ..." signals the beginning of a fairy tale. Images of damsels in distress, knights in shining armor, and the prerequisite enchanted forest have become expected fare in this genre. Romantics who wrote fairy tales, however, dismissed this stereotype, relegating it to folktales (*Volksmärchen*), associated with peasants and children. Such tales had little in common with what the Romantics called "art fairy tales" (*Kunstmärchen*). This distinction began among the German Romantics who defined the *Kunstmärchen* as a form reaching beyond the simple folktale or childhood fantasy to encompass the Romantic search for the Infinite. The genre explored the fantastic or supernatural elements that existed in the world and how they could help unravel the mysteries surrounding human existence. Romantic fairy tales often investigated the human relationship between God and the devil. The tales involved a hero wandering in search of final answers, who encounters wonders on his journey.[1]

Another form of short fiction the Romantics specialized in was the novella. Its roots go back to medieval Italy, where short, well-crafted, often bawdy stories described local events, for example,

Boccaccio's *Decameron* (written between 1348 and 1353). The novella's realistic content influenced the development of short stories and novels. While Romantics regarded both the fairy tale and the novella as important forms of short fiction, they distinguished between the two. The fairy tale, in which the hero seeks spiritual meaning in the supernatural, never describes a specific place or time. Unlike the fairy tale, the novella exists in the here and now, in identifiable places. The hero searches for morality at the personal level and in wider society.[2]

The novella's great offspring, the novel officially came into its own during the Romantic era. While some commentaries regard Cervantes's *Don Quixote* (1605, Part II, 1615) as the first European novel, most discussions begin with the epistolary (a series of letters) novels of mid-eighteenth century Britain, such as Samuel Richardson's (1689–1761) *Pamela* (1740). In the latter half of the eighteenth century, theoretical discussions about the novel in Britain distanced it from "romances" (medieval tales of chivalry) and endorsed its realistic approach to telling stories of the past.[3] Romantics Friedrich Schlegel and Sir Walter Scott contributed to this discussion.

Schlegel argued that, despite national differences, important characteristics connected contemporary novels. He suggested the novel was universal because it could incorporate other genres such as poetry and drama. It could be considered a form of poetry because it too could "transform the soul." It was definitely connected to the romance insofar as the novel was a "story of love." In a 1789 essay "On Goethe's *Meister*," Schlegel acknowledged Goethe's novel *Wilhelm Meister's Years of Apprenticeship* as auguring a new direction in fiction. Schlegel, taken with Goethe's paced description of Wilhelm Meister's character, recognized a *Bildungsroman* (a novel of moral or psychological development) even before the genre had been identified. Goethe's model can be found in the works of many Romantic authors, including Jane Austen and Sir Walter Scott.[4]

Scott also shared his thoughts about novels. He endorsed them because they entertained with their well-constructed plots and often flamboyant characters. Scott defended the genre in Romantic terms as he highlighted its capacity to explore wide-ranging emotions, contrasts of human experience, and the search for balance.[5] He marked the distinction between romances and historical novels by suggesting the former explored manners, whereas the latter examined men. The study of manners, for him, appeared to be a frivolous endeavor, whereas the study of man provided access to timeless values.[6]

The Romantic novel developed four subgenres: the Gothic, the domestic, the national, and the historical. Horace Walpole's (1717–1797) *The Castle of Otranto* (1765) served as the genesis of the

Gothic novel, a mystery complete with haunted castle and supernatural occurrences. The Gothic novel flourished during the 1790s but was definitely passé by 1820. The domestic novel, which explored the values associated with middle-class life, emerged toward the end of the eighteenth century. This form began with Oliver Goldsmith's (1730?–1774) *The Vicar of Wakefield* (1766), but the identifiable antecedents to Romanticism's domestic fiction were the novels of Frances Burney (1752–1840), *Evelina* (1778) and *Camilla* (1796). The novels were written primarily for a female audience and often had young girls or women as central characters. Usually set in rural surroundings, domestic novels traced the heroine's search for both her true identity and the perfect husband. Maria Edgeworth (1767–1849) and Jane Austen (1775–1817) are recognized as successful authors of domestic fiction.[7]

The national and historical novels of the Age of Romanticism have a close relationship, because they have a similar goal—to enhance a people's national identity and pride. The national "tales" often refer to a "past" that may have been sentimentally contrived, for example the "democracy" practiced by England's medieval barons and knights.[8] Maria Edgeworth's and Sydney Owenson, Lady Morgan's (1783?–1859) novels dominate any discussion of national "tales." In an attempt to demystify Ireland for English readers, these authors stressed the emotions of the central characters at the expense of "historical time." Sir Walter Scott, the individual most closely associated with the historical novel, addressed Scotland's historic past, where the central characters remain marginal to the wider discussion of cultural clashes and changes.[9]

Like Scott, many Romantic dramatists looked to the past for inspiration, such as William Shakespeare's (1564–1616) works. The "rediscovery" of the bard occurred because of the Romantic rebellion against Classicism's imposed rules. The Schlegel brothers articulated this view. For example, August Wilhelm defined Romantic drama by noting that the Classical form had been unified, harmonious, and artificial, whereas Romantic drama evinced a duality—"this worldly" versus "other worldly"—and a variety not found in Classical drama. He also noted the importance of cultivating patriotism through plays and felt that Shakespeare's historical dramas should serve as models to emulate.[10]

The passions unleashed by the French Revolution and its aftermath served as the stimulus for many dramatists. Their desire to break with Classicism's rules led many to write lengthy works often with political themes. Virtually none of these plays was produced, and those that were, proved unsuccessful. The problem with the dramas rested on two issues. First, most were too detailed and, therefore, too long to produce on stage. Second, the language, used by Shelley for example, did not fit the theatre audience's prevailing taste. This audience wanted to be entertained, which led to the growing popularity of the melodrama, characterized by romance, violent action, and the triumph of virtue.[11]

The Germans

Friedrich Schlegel set the tone for Romantic fiction as he decried the depiction of the ordinary, intoning that it was the author's responsibility to deal with the everyday only insofar as it led to the exploration of the Infinite. Schlegel wrote one semi-autobiographical novel, *Lucinde* (1799), which explores the passions of a young couple and introduces many themes that would influence subsequent Romantics. Like Rousseau's *Julie, or The New Eloise* and Goethe's *The Sorrows of Young Werther*, the plot revolves around a young man who falls in love with a married woman. But unlike the earlier novels, *Lucinde* ends with the triumph of true love, albeit in a partnership unsanctioned by the sacrament of marriage. The protagonists view their relationship, although illicit in society's eyes, as an "authentic marriage" because their love is both spiritual and sensual.[12]

German prose authors took Schlegel's advice to heart and often turned to the fantastic as a way to explore humanity's universal dilemmas. They eschewed the realism practiced by English authors such as Jane Austen and, therefore, produced no great Romantic novels.

Novalis, for example, fully absorbed Schlegel's injunction to explore the Infinite and did so in his poetry (see Chapter 2) and in his prose. His essay "Christianity or Europe" (1826), written in 1799, discussed the medieval past where reason and nature peacefully coexisted. In Novalis's version of history, the medieval world enjoyed harmony because all Europeans shared the same faith, Roman Catholic Christianity. But the Protestant Reformation and the emergence of rationalism associated with the Scientific Revolution and the Enlightenment caused confusion. The French Revolution contributed to the death of the old world, but created a meaningless world in its wake. Neither the Papacy nor Protestant church leaders could heal society's wounds. This task would fall to a new Christianity which would unite Europe in true peace and happiness independent of any organized church. This harmony would come from a higher spiritual state, a new mysticism that used human intuition to discover God.[13]

Novalis, in true Romantic fashion, explores the theme of love and how it affects the poet's creativity in his novel, *Heinrich von*

Ofterdingen (1802). Set in the Middle Ages, the young hero Heinrich, an aspiring *Minnesänger* (minstrel), embarks on a journey. He experiences a dream in which he sees the mysterious blue flower that embodies the Infinite to which all poets aspire. He continues, and upon reaching his grandfather's home, he meets a young woman with whom he falls in love. Her death unleashes a new journey. Although Novalis died before finishing the novel, his notes indicate that Heinrich would escape reality and experience mystical unity with the Infinite. He will be crowned king of the *Minnesänger*, will discover the blue flower, and will be reunited with his lost love. The moral highlights the triumph of poetry and love over the rational world.[14]

Novalis died in 1801 and the publication of his works fell to Friedrich Schlegel and Ludwig Tieck (1773–1853), his literary companions. As an author, Tieck excelled in the shorter prose genres, the *Kunstmärchen* ("art fairy tales") and the novella, but he also wrote a novel and several dramas. Tieck wanted his *Kunstmärchen* to confront the issues of human existence. In *Der gestiefelte Kater* (*Puss in Boots* [1797]), he created a play which is a three-act fairy tale. The plot describes the adventures of Gottlieb, a poor peasant, and his talking cat. The latter orchestrates matters so that Gottlieb marries a princess. In the play, Tieck reaches beyond the conventional fairy tale; during the drama's performance, the actors step out of character and ask the audience its opinion about the story. Despite Tieck's claims that he wanted the audience to return to childhood, he essentially hoped to provoke ideas about challenging conventional rules.[15]

As with many Romantic works, Tieck's novel, *Franz Sternbalds Wanderungen* (*Franz Sternbald's Travels* [1798]) is set in the sixteenth century and recounts the story of a young man, who aspires to become a painter. He sets out for Italy to learn the craft and reconnects with a young woman whom he had met as a child. Franz struggles with his passion for her and faces the great dilemma—will he lose his artistic inspiration if his muse (the beloved) actually becomes his lover?[16]

While Tieck wrote novellas, novels, and dramas, his contemporary E. T. A. Hoffmann's (1776–1822) primary legacy rests with his famous tales where he examines the artist and his relationship to the world. (See Primary Document 9.) Hoffmann admitted his debt to Tieck since he had been the one to elevate the fairy tale to true literature.[17] Moreover, Hoffmann's novel *Die Elixiere des Teufels* (*The Devil's Elixir* [1815–1816]) explores a popular Romantic theme: that man's fate is not in his hands. The novel tells the story of a monk who breaks his vows and commits crimes, culminating in the murder of his half brother. The mechanism that leads the monk astray is a devil's potion. He is briefly redeemed by a young girl and confesses his sins, but he is still condemned because of his father's crimes, which had led to God's curse upon him and all his descendents.[18]

Hoffmann's heroes were often troubled artists seeking inspiration, who confronted the Romantic artist's dilemma: is it better to have a distant muse and be inspired or possess her and lose all? This question forms the plot of Hoffmann's best-known work, *Der Sandmann* (*The Sand Man* [1817]). The novella begins with unusual goings-on, connected with a mysterious nocturnal visitor called the Sand Man and the hero's father. One night Nathanael discovers the Sand Man's identity, and when threatened not to reveal it, lapses into a coma. Shortly thereafter, an explosion kills his father. Nathanael goes off to university, leaving his sweetheart Clara behind. He buys and uses a magical telescope whose maker controls the will of the person looking through it. Nathanael espies a beautiful young girl, his professor's daughter Olimpia, and promptly forgets Clara.

It is revealed that Olimpia is an automaton—a creation of the professor's in collaboration with the Sand Man. Nathanael breaks down and returns home where an inheritance and returned health appear to bode well for him. But in the final scene, he and Clara, now his wife, have climbed to the top of the town hall tower. She calls attention to the distant view and he pulls out the telescope for a better look. His madness returns and he tries to throw her off, but she is rescued by her brother, and Nathanael then commits suicide.[19] His psychological disintegration provides a modern exploration of the human psyche.

The British

The novel prevails in any discussion of Romantic prose in Britain, where Gothic, domestic, national, and historical examples are readily found. Women authors dominated the first three types, and the best-selling novelists specialized in Gothic romances. These mystery stories, often with ruined castles as backdrops, explored the plight of young heroines who often battled society's dictum that they must submit to the will of their male elders or that of institutions that wished to keep women in their proper place. A Romantic theme common to such works involves a contest between good and evil. At times the supernatural plays a role, but then again, mysterious sounds in the middle of the night were often explained by ordinary events.[20]

The queen of Gothic fiction, Ann Ward Radcliffe (1764–1823), wrote nine novels between 1789 and 1797. Her fourth, *The Mysteries of Udolfo* (1794), remains the best known. *Udolfo* has all the characteristics of Gothic fiction: set in late sixteenth-century France and Italy, the young heroine, Emily, has loving parents who die early in the story. She becomes the ward of her father's sister, Madame Cheron, who hinders Emily's liaison with her true love, the nobleman Valancourt. After the aunt marries Count Montoni, the three eventually move to his forbidding Castle Udolfo. Various mysteries surround the castle, including the sightings of ghostly apparitions. (See Primary Document 10.) Emily escapes to France, where she returns to the convent in which she had taken refuge shortly after her father's death. Eventually, she and Valancourt are reunited.

Not all female novelists emulated Ann Radcliffe's Gothic style. Jane Austen, who dominated the field of domestic novels, pointedly made fun of the Gothic novel in *Northanger Abbey* (1818). Austen became familiar with Gothic fiction because her father enjoyed Radcliffe's novels. Apparently, Austen found this genre silly, especially when the young heroines always fainted whenever something frightening happened. Her spoof follows the Gothic format: the heroine, Catherine Moreland, needs to make a proper marriage. She is misrepresented as being an heiress and suddenly finds suitors. One candidate inhabits an abbey, which Catherine visits. Because she has read *The Mysteries of Udolfo*, she envisions the abbey as a place of mystery, but finds it clean and airy. In looking for clues of a supposed murder, Catherine discovers two old trunks. She is almost beside herself when she finds bed linens in one and a maid's laundry list in the other. Her suitor then makes fun of her and the fanciful notions that Gothic novels have placed in her head. In satirizing Gothic heroines and their fates, Austen accomplished three things. Not only did she create a story about growing up and losing youthful delusions, but she also provided a warning about how girls' superficial education produced impractical and overly sentimental creatures who often lived in a fantasy world rather than in reality. She also criticized a society where power was tied to wealth as it led to deceit in the quest for entrance into that world.[21]

Jane Austen's distinction in Romantic literature, of course, rests with her domestic novels. Most of her great works were written in the 1790s, but had to wait until years later to be published. They include such classics as *Sense and Sensibility* (1811), *Pride and Prejudice* (1813), *Mansfield Park* (1814), and *Emma* (1816), which were published anonymously.

The propensity for women to publish works anonymously was followed by Mary Wollstonecraft Godwin Shelley (1797–1851), who wrote about the search for the godlike power of creating life in

Frankenstein, the best-known novel written by a woman during the Age of Romanticism. Her predecessors in Gothic fiction liberally used mysterious castles and hidden identities to propel their plots. Shelley's style incorporates terror of a psychological nature.[22] The story explores Victor Frankenstein's obsession with science and, in particular, how to create life. He succeeds, but Victor cannot love or nurture his creature, which initially is childlike in its naiveté. The monster secretly educates himself but is rejected because he is big and ugly. He grows angry with his creator/father and seeks revenge against the entire Frankenstein family and Victor especially by killing everyone close to him. (See Primary Document 11.) Victor cannot deal psychologically with what he has done and slowly becomes deranged. He wants to destroy the monster and chases him to the Arctic, where Victor, near death, encounters an ice-bound ship, tells his tortured story, and then dies. The monster is left wandering the polar ice cap, seeking death.

While Gothic fiction embodied the Romantic wish to answer the great questions of life, the national tale addressed another intellectual current: the search for ethnic identity. While Maria Edgeworth's *Castle Rackrent* (1800) is credited with being the first national tale, Sydney Owenson, Lady Morgan's *The Wild Irish Girl* (1806) had a greater impact on nineteenth-century Irish nationalism. In the novel, a dissolute young Englishman, Mortimer, is exiled to Ireland to mend his ways. It is as if he has time-traveled to a distant place and time. Gradually, his prejudices against Ireland wane, especially because of his growing attachment to the wild Irish girl, Glorvina.[23]

Whereas Owenson's novel represents the national tale, her contemporary Sir Walter Scott's specialty was the historical novel. Prompted by antiquarianism, Scott collected tales of his native Scotland. Already a recognized poet by 1813, Scott "rediscovered" a copy of a manuscript he had begun eight years earlier. Set in Scotland in 1745, it explored the ancient way of life of the Highland Scots with their clan traditions and warrior mentality and how it clashed with and eventually lost out to the encroaching modern, rational world embodied by the shopkeepers of the Lowlands and their values.[24]

The novel *Waverley* (1814) traces the adventures of young Englishman Edward Waverley. Upon his father becoming a widower, Edward lives primarily at his uncle's home. Although Edward's father supported the German Hanoverian dynasty, new to the British throne, his uncle retains Jacobite (supporters of the deposed Stuart dynasty) leanings. Like many young men of his social standing, at the appropriate age Edward receives an army commission and is sent to Scotland. Although essentially committing treason, he aligns himself with the Jacobite cause. He is found out and dismissed from his regiment. His romantic sensibilities, however, have been kindled, and he joins with Bonnie Prince Charlie in what Edward recognizes is a doomed cause. Of the two female interests in Edward's life, he eventually marries Rose Bradwardine, who embodies the world of contemporary Scotland, rather than Flora MacIvor, who represents the passions of the Highland clans of the past. Like Maria Edgeworth and Sydney Owenson, Lady Morgan, Scott wished to demystify Scotland for his English readers as those women had done for Ireland. He liked writing about the past because the facts of history were real. He could use the backdrop of that reality against which to create characters who led romantic and intriguing lives.[25]

Romantic writers also investigated madness: what caused it, and how did it affect human behavior? Scottish playwright and poet Joanna Baillie (1762–1851) confronted this theme in her fiction where she explored her characters' psychological states through dialogue and descriptions of their interactions with others.[26] In 1798, she published anonymously the initial *A Series of Plays on the Passions*, which included three blank verse dramas that described how the passions dictate human behavior. The work also included an "Introductory Discourse" in which Baillie argues that all literary genres should be written in "natural" language and the stories should discuss "realistic" events. She simultaneously criticizes the elite language of Classical literature and the supernatural flourishes of Gothic fiction.[27]

Baillie's dramas explore motivation, so her characters and ideas predominate over the plots. *De Monfort* (1798) tells the story of a young nobleman in medieval Germany. Jealousy has made De Monfort crazy, and although he tries to stop himself, he kills his rival. He then realizes his victim was not his enemy; rather De Monfort has deluded himself into believing this lie. With almost surgical precision, Baillie dissects De Monfort and his breakdown. The way she depicts human fears reveals her conscious exploration of the sublime.[28]

The French

While the British authors dominated the novel, French writers produced all forms of prose and often developed themes related to the changing political circumstances of their nation. The French Romantics explored opposites: nationalism versus cosmopolitanism, nature versus the city, religion versus secularism, and rationalism versus irrationalism. They initially focused on such discussions because society had been deeply scarred by the French Revolution and its aftermath and because such themes enabled them to elude royal censors.[29]

French Romanticism flourished in the 1820s, but its roots begin with diplomat and author Vicomte de Chateaubriand (1768–1848). An impoverished noble who grew up in a half-ruined medieval castle and left school to become a cavalry officer, he is recognized as France's first Romantic author. When the French Revolution broke out, he could not as a royalist remain in France, so in 1791, he traveled to North America where he spent time with trappers in the wilderness. After living in London from 1793 to 1800 and struggling to support himself by translating and teaching French, he returned to Paris and worked as a freelance journalist. It was at this time that his novel fragment *Atala* (1801) appeared. Reminiscent of Rousseau's *Julie, or The New Eloise*, it tells the story of a Native American girl whose mother takes a vow of chastity on her daughter's behalf. After a stranger comes to live among her tribe, Atala falls in love with him and eventually kills herself rather than break the vow. Besides the love story, Chateaubriand's beautiful descriptions of nature in the North American wilderness appealed to his readers. While *Atala* reflects the Romantic fascination with nature, Chateaubriand's other major work, *The Genius of Christianity* (1802), confronts another important theme: religion. In the novel, he describes a young man totally cut off from his world because of a lack of faith. The hero eventually turns to the Roman Catholic Church for solace. Like other Romantics, Chateaubriand returned to Christianity himself after youthful disillusionment with religion.[30] For Romanticism, Chateaubriand's importance rests with his masterful descriptions of nature in all its beauty and grandeur and its sharp contrast with the inner suffering of humans and their search for faith.

Another important early French Romantic was Anne Louise Germaine Necker, Madame de Staël (1766–1817), who wrote novels, plays, poetry, essays on politics and morals, literary criticism, history, and autobiography. Her major contribution to Romanticism, *Germany* (1810), was written after a tour of Germany in the winter of 1803–1804. She not only praised German character and culture but also attacked the repressive intellectual environment of Napoleonic France.[31] (See Primary Document 12.) According to de Staël, the Germans enjoyed a Romantic setting in which they freely engaged in the pursuit of individual feelings. Moreover, the artistic freedom the Germans enjoyed occurred because Germany was not a unified nation, whereas highly centralized France controlled its literary expression. She believed France's culture suffered because of the rigid guidelines dictated by Classicism.

A second-generation French Romantic, Victor Hugo (1802–1885), poet, playwright, and novelist, made vital contributions to Romanticism. His literary works explore man's dual nature of good and evil and address issues of political power and social inequality. Beyond his fiction, Hugo added to literary theory when he defined Romantic drama in the "Preface" to his drama *Cromwell* (1827). (See Primary Document 13.) He endorsed the Romantic tendency to explore opposites, such as good and evil or paganism versus Christianity. He continued the debate between Classicism and Romanticism in his verse drama *Hernani* (1831).[32] Passions ran so high at a performance, audience members started a brawl because of their differences over the old versus the new drama.

Hugo excelled in all genres including the novel and was inspired by Sir Walter Scott's *Waverley*, which was extremely popular in France. This model caused French writers to turn to great historical themes rather than concentrate on the plight of the individual. Whether in *The Hunchback of Notre Dame* (1813) or *Les Misérables* (1862), Hugo explored the human struggle with good and evil and other contradictions such as beauty versus ugliness and laughter versus tears. Hugo's other important quality was the clarity of his writing; he wrote with simplicity and a power that touched his readers.[33]

Another French Romantic, George Sand (Amandine Aurore Dupin, Madame Dudevant [1804–1876]), merits mention. Her first novel, *Indiana* (1832), brought her immediate fame. It tells the story of a young girl bound against her will in an unhappy marriage who abandons her husband and finds true love. It attacks the society that condoned such marriages, such as the one from which Sand herself had escaped. Her subsequent novels continued the discussion of freedom for women but also dealt with social and class relationships and more specifically with social reform. When the Revolution of 1848 broke out in February, Sand, still an idealist, wrote propaganda about the revolution's goals and served as a behind-the-scenes advisor to the government, then led by Romantic poet Alphonse Lamartine (1790–1869). When a group of feminists requested that she vie for a seat in the General Assembly, she refused. She maintained that women should only get involved in politics in the future after society had been radically transformed.

The Italians

The greatest Italian writer of the Romantic era, Alessandro Manzoni (1785–1873), included historical events and political themes in his poetry and novels. Manzoni felt his task was to provide a cultural identity for Italy. His masterpiece, *The Betrothed* (1827), is a sweeping historical novel full of romance and passion that also describes Italian society where the peasants were at the mercy of powerful Spanish lords. (See Primary Document 14.) Set in the seventeenth century, the novel tells the story of two peasant lovers, Renzo and Lucca, kept apart by Don' Roderigo, the conniving local lord, and the ineffectual parish priest Father Cristoforo. The plot serves as an indictment of the powerful exploiting and tyrannizing the weak. In the novel, Manzoni's Italian patriotism, concern for the poor, and a Christian perspective can be discerned. In 1842, he rewrote the entire novel in the Tuscan dialect, in order to promote it as the literary language of Italy. His was an important legacy as he used Italy's powerful past to invoke activism in the present.[34]

As with Romantic poetry, prose and drama of the era confront the issues that humanity faced in a time of upheaval. The subjects of these works explore how people coped with challenges, confronted the unknown, and handled the eternal theme of love. The plight of the misunderstood or marginalized artist reappears as well. Romantic prose and drama, more so than poetry, present issues that ordinary people experienced and how they sought to find happiness. These works often engaged with the issues of the day, including emerging national identities.

Notes

1. James Trainor, "The Märchen," in *The Romantic Period in Germany*, ed. Siegbert Prawer (New York: Schocken Books, 1970), 97–99; Marianne Thalmann, *The Romantic Fairy Tale: Seeds of Surrealism* (Ann Arbor: University of Michigan Press, 1964), 33–35.

2. Brian Rowley, "The Novelle," in *The Romantic Period in Germany*, 121–123, 128.

3. Marshall Brown, "Theory of the Novel," in *The Cambridge History of Literary Criticism, Vol. 5, Romanticism* (New York: Cambridge University Press, 2000), 252; John Sutherland, "The Novel," in *A Companion to Romanticism*, ed. Duncan Wu (Malden, MA: Blackwell, 2001), 337.

4. Brown, "Theory of the Novel," 257–261, 263–264, 266–267.

5. Ibid., 268, 270.

6. Corinna Russell, "The Novel," in *Romanticism: An Oxford Guide*, ed. Nicholas Roe (New York: Oxford University Press, 2005), 376–377.

7. Sutherland, "The Novel," 339–341.

8. Ibid., 341–342.

9. Ina Ferris, *The Achievement of Literary Authority: Gender, History, and the Waverley Novels* (Ithaca, NY: Cornell University Press, 1991), 105, 117–118, 129.

10. Roger Paulin, "The Drama," in *The Romantic Period in Germany*, 175–176, 178.

11. Ibid., 183; Frederick Burwick, "The Romantic Drama," in *A Companion to Romanticism*, 323–324, 326–328.

12. Hans Eichner, "The Novel," in *The Romantic Period in Germany*, 91–93.

13. Max Blechman, "The Revolutionary Dream of Early German Romanticism," in *Revolutionary Romanticism* (San Francisco: City Lights Books, 1999), 13–14; Morse Peckham, *The Birth of Romanticism 1790 to 1815* (Greenwood, FL: Penkeville Publishing Co., 1986), 138–140.

14. Eichner, "The Novel," 79.

15. Isaiah Berlin, *The Roots of Romanticism* (Princeton, NJ: Princeton University Press, 1999), 114, 116.

16. Eichner, "The Novel," 75, 77–78.

17. Thalmann, *The Romantic Fairy Tale*, 88–90.

18. Eichner, "The Novel," 87–89.

19. Rowley, "The Novelle," 132–133.

20. Diane Long Hoeveler, *Gothic Feminism: The Professionalization of Gender from Charlotte Smith to the Brontës* (University Park, PA: Penn State University Press, 1998), 5–6, 186.

21. Hoeveler, *Gothic Feminism*, 127–143; Anne K. Mellor, *Romanticism and Gender* (New York: Routledge, 1993), 63–64.

22. David Miall, "Gothic Fiction," in *A Companion to Romanticism*, 352–353.

23. Ferris, *The Achievement of Literary Authority*, 122–123, 125–133.

24. David Morse, *Romanticism: A Structural Analysis* (Totowa, NJ: Barnes and Noble, 1982), 148–149.

25. Ferris, *The Achievement of Literary Authority*, 120–121.

26. Janice Patten, "Joanna Baillie, A Series of Plays," in *A Companion to Romanticism*, 171–172; Burwick, "The Romantic Drama," 329.

27. Stuart Curran, "The I Altered," in *Romanticism and Feminism*, ed. Anne K. Mellor (Bloomington: Indiana University Press, 1988), 185–186; Patten, "Joanna Baillie," 170; Marlon B. Ross, *The Contours of Masculine Desire: Romanticism and the Rise of Women's Poetry* (New York: Oxford University Press, 1989), 285–286.

28. Patten, "Joanna Baillie," 173–175.

29. Frank Paul Bowman, "The Specificity of French Romanticism," in *The People's Vision*, ed. Andrea Ciccarelli et al. (Melbourne: Monash University, 1999), 74–88.

30. Maurice Cranston, *The Romantic Movement* (Cambridge, MA: Blackwell, 1994), 80–81; Peckham, *The Birth of Romanticism*, 104–105, 168.

31. Cranston, *The Romantic Movement*, 77–79; Peckham, *The Birth of Romanticism*, 273–275.

32. Albert W. Halsall, *Victor Hugo and the Romantic Drama* (Buffalo, NY: University of Toronto Press, 1998), 64–68.

33. Cranston, *The Romantic Movement*, 79, 88–89, 92–93, 95–96.

34. Ibid., 109–115.

CHAPTER 4

ROMANTIC PAINTING

The Romantic need for personal expression found the perfect outlet in painting. Like the literary Romantics, artists recognized the transitional nature of their era and expressed it through their creative efforts. In *ancien régime* Europe, painters needed to find wealthy, aristocratic patrons to support them, and because of this dependence, artistic efforts had to be channeled into styles dictated by official art academies, but the social and economic changes occurring at the turn of the nineteenth century led to a new dynamic in the art world. Middle-class connoisseurs and museums now purchased paintings, drawings, and sculptures. While many artists continued traditional styles, others experimented with techniques and themes.

Romantic Art and Artists

Although the decorative arts include drawing, painting, sculpture, and architecture, here the focus will be select Romantic painters and their works. Of the arts, painting is regarded as the most Romantic because it is two-dimensional, and through intangibles such as a sense of space or light it creates an emotional tone which reflects the Romantic quest for the Infinite. By contrast, sculpture and architecture are three-dimensional and have physical presence. These objects may be beautiful, but one never escapes their mass, and for the Romantics, this characteristic made them less awesome.[1]

The painters consciously sensed the new directions in which they were taking their art: themes included the beauty of nature, the importance of imagination over reason, and a fascination with the past, the mysterious, and the exotic. Works of art, they argued, should come from the artist's soul and not merely copy what has come before. They regarded their efforts, especially small sketches, as personal reflections, similar to poetry and music. The Romantic painters' principal genre was landscapes. The technical perfection associated with Classical landscapes gave way to some Romantics' experimentation with light and its effects. These painters carefully chose their colors to appeal to the emotions, and they depicted nature so it would spiritually affect the viewer. The first attempts at such expression occurred in Scandinavia and in the German lands.[2]

Romantic painters preferred themes related to a new view about human history. The Romantics saw history as continuous; the past, present, and future were connected, but unlike Enlightenment thinkers, the Romantics did not see history as the story of inevitable human progress. They rebelled against the *philosophes'* critical judgments of peoples of earlier times. Each society, pagan, Judeo-Christian, Islamic, European, non-European, must be valued on its own merits. As a result, Romantic painters explored themes associated with the past and a variety of world cultures.[3]

Romantic painters often used the Middle Ages as a setting, in part, because of the spiritual crises many faced. They sought to reclaim their spirituality by creating an idealized vision of the medieval world as a time of religious harmony. Also, some Romantics were drawn to the pomp and ceremony of Roman Catholic religious ritual. Moreover, Protestant churches were plain when contrasted with medieval cathedrals with their statues and stained glass windows. The Romantics believed the beautiful objects and settings associated with Roman Catholicism could bring people together as a community.[4]

Artists also turned to exotic peoples and places: maybe in such locales the journey of self-discovery and search for a better way of life could be found. Some visited Africa and the Middle East in search of inspiration, whereas others had to be armchair travelers, entertained by the exotic as described, for example, by Lord Byron in *Childe Harold's Pilgrimage*. The mystery and ferocity often associated with exotic lands can be found in many Romantic paintings.

The hero became another favorite theme for Romantic artists. Tied to the concept of individual freedom and the imperative to be true to the self, Romantic painters viewed heroes as the ultimate examples of personal accomplishment. Napoleon was a favorite but paradoxical subject. In an era which proclaimed liberty and equality, his actions led to the loss of freedom for many people. After Napoleon's defeat and exile to St. Helena, he remained a hero—especially because the Romantics seemed fond of lost causes.[5]

Romantic artists also explored the psyche because many were obsessed with dreams and their insights about both the past and the future. Many Romantics felt that while dreaming, the individual could return to mankind's lost unity. Also, more than a century before Sigmund Freud (1856–1939), author of *Interpretation of*

Dreams (1900), Romantic painters such as Henry Fuseli (1741–1825) depicted erotic themes that occurred during dreams. His painting, *The Nightmare* (1781), shows a sleeping woman draped across a bed with a gargoyle seated on her chest while a stallion with wild eyes and flared nostrils leers from behind the curtains. This painting strongly suggests sexual themes.[6]

As with the literary Romantics, the artists saw themselves as the spokesmen for their age. They believed the artist's creative imagination allowed him to have insights about the world denied ordinary men. Because some challenged established cultural traditions, it made them automatically outsiders—a trait they shared with their literary counterparts. Other Romantics avoided compromising with the traditional styles by conveniently dying young.[7]

Turner and Constable

Considered a great landscape painter, Joseph Mallord William Turner (1775–1851) dominates discussions of Romantic art. In his masterpieces, such as the *Burning of the Houses of Lords and Commons* (1835), he experimented with light, color, and atmosphere, and foreshadowed the late nineteenth century revolution in art known as Impressionism. He entered the Royal Academy's art school at fourteen and because of his academy training his early paintings tend to be traditional in style. He began around 1800 to copy paintings by the Old Masters to improve his technique, but he came to reject the restrictions his instructors placed upon him.[8] In 1802, he toured Italy and France and studied the seventeenth-century Dutch masters and their seascapes. As with his earlier efforts at mimicking the Old Masters and now the Dutch, Turner practiced a traditional landscape approach. Shortly thereafter, it became evident that he was developing a unique style. Turner, who liked to wander the countryside seeking inspiration, began to paint outdoors. Usually, European artists at that time would do pencil sketches outside, but painting was done in a studio. Turner wanted nature to inspire him and influence how and what he painted.

He chose dramatic subjects and then painted with an imprecision so that, even though they could be understood, what caught the viewer was the paint's luminosity and how Turner attempted to portray atmospheric conditions, for example, the howling winds associated with a snowstorm or a major storm at sea. *Snowstorm: Hannibal and His Army Crossing the Alps* (1812) illustrates this technique. The caravan of Hannibal's forces and the mighty elephants on their way to invade Roman territory are diminished to almost nothing because of the storm's fury.[9] Critics attacked Turner's later paintings because they exhibited a "lack of finish." They disliked his style of bold brush strokes and dabs of paint which, although not totally abstract, did not have the precision that contemporary taste demanded. Although Turner's paintings offended some, knowledgeable critics did recognize his strengths.[10] Turner's bold brush work and choice of subject matter highlight his connection to Romanticism. Turner wished to make examining a painting an ecstatic experience for the viewer. He directly confronted the sublime in his paintings, finding special inspiration from fire and water, which, when stirred up, manifested incredible force. Turner's experiments with light, color, and atmosphere left an important legacy that subsequent modern artists have emulated.[11]

In terms of style, no painter could be more distinct from Turner than John Constable (1776–1837). A landscape painter, too, Constable's works evoke a peacefulness and harmony not found in Turner's. As a child, Constable loved to draw, and at nineteen, he decided to become a painter. It took four years for him to secure an appointment to the Royal Academy where he spent seven years in technical training. Like other academically trained painters, Constable studied the Old Masters, but only the Dutch landscapes and seascapes really appealed to him.[12]

Between 1802 and 1806, when not painting portraits to earn money, Constable focused on drawings and oil sketches of the countryside. His sketches in open air on sheets of paper were meant as preparatory efforts for studio-done oils. Although none of these oil sketches seemed out of the ordinary, they showed Constable's painstaking commitment to detail. He did not just reproduce what he had seen, rather he conveyed the emotions associated with that view.[13] The sketches and subsequent great oils that he produced after 1809 reveal his insight about painting nature. He often sketched the same scene countless times, and with each effort subtle changes emerged. For Constable, each sketch represented the coming together of a specific moment in time and the artist's perception of it.[14]

Constable began painting large canvases, what he called his six footers, after 1817. He did a series of six paintings: *The White Horse, Stratford Mill, The Hay Wain, View of the Stour near Dedham, The Lock,* and *The Leaping Horse* (1819–1824). The most famous, *The Hay Wain* (1821), shows a cottage along the Stour River, near which a farm boy guides a horse-drawn wagon or "wain" in the shallow river while a dog looks on. A fisherman appears near his boat while a woman draws water. The picture captures high noon in the countryside, full of detail, color, and activity, but it is, nevertheless, serene. As one critic noted, the painting is "alive with incident."[15]

The death of Constable's wife in 1826 left him depressed, but he continued painting landscapes which tended to get darker and more intense in color. Works such as *Hadleigh Castle* (1829) date from this time. The darker tones, especially in the skies of the later paintings, may reflect his personal sorrow. They could also convey his response to the economic hardships that rural England had been facing because of the recession and depopulation.[16] Like his fellow Romantics, Constable idealized nature. He painted rural scenes that recalled an idyllic past. Constable wanted his paintings to create a moral feeling, to uplift viewers and remind them of an earlier, more harmonious time. His nostalgia for the "good old days" clearly ties him to his fellow Romantics.[17]

Constable, who saw a divine purpose in nature, believed it was not enough for the painter to reproduce what existed; he had to act as its interpreter. In this respect, Constable's views sound much like William Wordsworth's, with very good reason. Constable had read Wordsworth's then unpublished poem, *The Prelude*, and identified with the role of the artist as the medium by which the divine in nature is conveyed to ordinary people.[18]

Friedrich and Runge

Germany produced two important Romantic landscape painters: Caspar David Friedrich and Philipp Otto Runge. Both strove to incorporate emotions into their art, but their landscapes were not serene like Constable's, rather, they were filled with awe, wonder, and magic. Caspar David Friedrich's (1774–1840) childhood included several personal tragedies, including his mother's death when he was seven and his brother's six years later. Some suggest the dark religiosity of his work stems from these childhood losses. After studying engraving and painting in Copenhagen from 1794 to 1798, he moved to Dresden, a center of artistic and cultural life, often referred to as the "Florence of Germany."[19] As with his fellow Romantics, Friedrich's travels to natural settings in northern Germany, the Baltic, and the Harz Mountains, inspired him. He knew nature well because one of the ways he earned a living was by making precise topographical sketches. His diary entries reflect his enthusiasm for natural scenes, especially the mountains. (See Primary Document 15.)

In his oil paintings, nature becomes the setting for religious experience. Many paintings depict monasteries in ruins or overrun cemeteries, the physical symbols of organized religion in decay. Friedrich's images convey the sense that even in the decline or absence of an organized church, man could fulfill his spiritual needs in nature. Personally, Friedrich believed painting nature was a form of worship.[20] The objects in Friedrich's paintings have specific meanings. For example, distant mountains stand for God; ships, the transition from this world to the next; blue sky, the promise of the resurrection; dead or dying oak trees, remnants of paganism in Christian Europe; Gothic church ruins, the failure of organized Christianity; and, the cross, Christianity.[21]

In his paintings, Friedrich did not reproduce a landscape exactly as it appeared. He would do a sketch on site, but in his studio, he often rearranged the setting to suit the mood he wished to convey. For example, to increase his viewer's fear of heights, Friedrich might make the slope of a mountain steeper than it actually was. Friedrich's landscapes and seascapes are vast in scope; if human figures appear, especially in his later works, they are small and anonymous. The formal art world recognized Friedrich and his talent after he completed *The Cross in the Mountains* (1808). Also known as the "Tetschen Altar," it depicts Jesus on the cross atop a rugged mountain at sunset. The overcast sky is illuminated by the sun's rays as it sets. The scene conveys isolation, but also the Christian message: sunset reflects the death of paganism in response to the Christian promise of hope, symbolized by the fir trees and the Crucifixion.[22]

In 1811, Friedrich sent nine paintings to an exhibition in Weimar where they were admired by among others Goethe and Ludwig Tieck. The conservative leaders of the Berlin Academy of Fine Arts, however, disliked Friedrich's work because of its unusual depiction of religion. He turned to nationalistic themes shortly thereafter in response to the war against Napoleon. Between 1812 and 1814, he produced several patriotic works, including *Graves of Ancient Heroes* (1812). In this work, the two figures, French soldiers, are dwarfed by the open tomb (a crevasse in the mountain side) and the monuments dedicated to fallen German heroes.[23]

Another Friedrich painting, *The Polar Sea* (1824), draws inspiration from an actual event, the shipwreck of Englishman William Edward Parry's expedition in 1820 while in search of a Northwest Passage from the Atlantic to the Pacific. Parry's ship became icebound, and when the ice began to break up, it crushed the ship. Although Friedrich had never seen polar ice, the painting captures the power, cold, and bleakness of the Arctic. The painting shows slabs of ice, pushed upward against each other, while parts of the crushed ship are barely visible and man is nowhere to be seen.

Friedrich's contemporary, Philipp Otto Runge (1777–1810), remained virtually unknown during his life. Regarded today as Germany's second greatest Romantic painter, Runge died at thirty-three, leaving a limited body of work. Nevertheless, his views about the role of the artist and his efforts to convey religious feeling through his paintings clearly establish his ties to Romanticism.[24] Runge began art studies in Copenhagen in 1799 where his training was traditional. After two years, he decided he could not learn anything new, and he moved to Dresden where he met the Schlegels, visited Friedrich, and dabbled in mystical philosophy. He relocated to Hamburg in 1804 where he produced his greatest paintings.

Runge believed he had to move beyond Classicism's formal rules to something new. He demanded realistic detail in his works, but they also had to have deeper meaning. For example, *The Hülsenbeck Children* (1805), a commissioned portrait, had much more to reveal than just two siblings pulling their baby brother in a wagon. The older children dominate the scene, while the baby appears almost as an afterthought since he is surrounded by huge sunflowers—clearly connecting childhood innocence to nature. Runge's best depictions of nature appear in his children's portraits, and he felt it important to constantly remind man of his place within nature.[25]

Runge's studies of mysticism led him to believe that flowers represent different facets of man's life. Because flowers go from seeds, to buds, to full blooms, then wither and die, they symbolize aspects of God's presence on earth and man's interrelatedness with creation. Flowers and small children appeared in his most ambitious work, *Times of the Day*. His goal was to produce four paintings representing various times of the day. Although he made engravings of all four scenes, he only painted two versions of *Morning*. *Morning* (1808) has a symmetrical balance: in the foreground against a natural, light-infused landscape, a baby opens his hands as if to greet the rising sun. He lies in a flower-covered meadow and cherubs hover over him while Venus, the morning star, rises into heaven. Cherubs and flowers also appear in the frame around the picture. Runge's baby and the cherubs represent human emotions in their most natural state. Here, Runge reveals his connection to the other Romantics who also shared his belief in children's innate spontaneity, genuineness, and innocence.[26] As with many Romantics, Runge sought to find God in nature. He believed nature's beauty served as God's highest revelation to humankind. Through his art, he combined spirituality and a deep appreciation of nature to create a bond between people and nature.

Géricault and Delacroix

The dominant figures of French Romantic painting are Théodore Géricault and Eugène Delacroix. Géricault lived a tragically short life, yet he left an amazing body of work which later influenced Delacroix's style. Jean-Louis-André-Théodore Géricault (1791–1824) chose to study with Pierre Narcisse Guérin (1774–1833), a Classical master, in 1810. Guérin taught Géricault the fundamentals, including how to create scenes on large canvases. Géricault was drawn to painting contemporary events rather than historical or mythological scenes. His first major work, *An Officer of the Chasseurs Commanding a Charge* (1812), depicts an officer, seated on a rearing horse with his sword drawn, near a smoking battlefield. Géricault captures the bravery and pride associated with the triumphant military. French critics and the public loved the painting because it alluded to Napoleon's victories. Géricault's interest in contemporary subjects eventually provoked a critical response. In 1814, he exhibited *Wounded Cuirassier Leaving the Field*, which shows a wounded soldier who anxiously looks over his shoulder as he leads his frightened horse. The public's mixed reactions can be understood because during the painting's initial showing Napoleon sat in exile on Elba. Also, the painting's dark colors appeared to echo defeat.

Géricault's masterpiece, *The Raft of the Medusa* (1819), also caused him anguish because of its lukewarm reception. This huge canvas (sixteen by twenty-three feet) depicts an overcrowded, storm-tossed raft; many aboard are dead or dying. Off in the distance, a ship can be seen, and the raft's passengers are madly trying to signal it but to no avail. Géricault based the painting on an event that had occurred three years earlier when a convoy of ships sailed to West Africa. One of them, the *Medusa*, ran aground, but it did not have enough lifeboats. A makeshift raft was loaded with one hundred fifty people to be towed to shore by the lifeboats. The raft was eventually cut adrift, and when found two weeks later, only fifteen people were still alive. The survivors admitted to acts of cannibalism. The initial accident had occurred because the *Medusa's* captain, a political appointee, was incompetent. After Géricault met one of the survivors, he worked on the painting for eighteen months, during which time he studied corpses to enhance the work's realism. The completed canvas presents incredible insight into human suffering.[27] The painting's less-than-enthusiastic reception occurred because Géricault depicted an event the government wished forgotten as it drew attention to political corruption.

During the remainder of his life, Géricault produced no further masterpieces although his technical skill appeared in a series of portraits he produced of mental patients. He suffered from the torment of being a rejected artist—a theme associated with the Age of Romanticism. He set the tone for subsequent Romantic artists, especially Eugène Delacroix, by choosing unusual themes and using bold colors and brush strokes.

The Salon exhibit of *The Massacre at Chios* by Ferdinand-Victor-Eugène Delacroix (1798–1863) occurred in 1824—the year Géricault died. The painting examined an historical event, the massacre of twenty thousand Greeks by Turks on the island of Chios. The victorious Turks' ferocity and the anguish of the dead and dying, especially the women and children, dominate this canvas. Although depicting a tragedy, the painting's clear lack of a moral statement led a contemporary critic to rename it "The Massacre of Painting."[28]

Like Géricault, Delacroix had studied with Pierre Narcisse Guérin as a teenager. At his studio, Delacroix met Géricault and came to appreciate his art. Later in 1825, Delacroix traveled to England and visited Turner and Constable. The Frenchman admired the English painting style with its freedom and flexibility and liked Constable's delicate technique and use of color. Delacroix came to realize that what in nature appears to be one color, actually comprises many shades and that the artist must replicate them in order to engage his viewer.

Between 1827 and 1832, Delacroix produced a series of masterpieces, many inspired by his passion for the Greeks and their War of Independence against Turkey. As a tribute to Byron, Delacroix painted *The Death of Sardanapalus* (1827) which was based on a scene from Byron's play that portrayed the suicide of the defeated Assyrian ruler. Although, in Byron's version, the man's death is noble, Delacroix chose another tack. His painting shows the virtually passive Assyrian reclining on his bed, surrounded by splendor, watching his harem executed. Delacroix, in order to evoke emotion, assaults his viewer in his depiction of the naked women, the violence of the attackers, and the ruler's excessive luxury.[29] The official Paris art world rejected this painting.

Normally, Delacroix did not use contemporary events as inspiration. However, in July 1830, France experienced another revolution, and King Charles X was deposed. Delacroix commemorated the event in *Liberty Leading the People* (1830), his most famous painting. It is more subdued than his earlier works: bare-breasted Liberty leads a motley group of rebels over the bodies of the defeated. When the painting appeared in the 1831 Salon exhibit, the middle-class audience did not appreciate the ruffians that Delacroix included as part of the revolutionary crowd. Nevertheless, the painting was regarded as a heroic depiction of the revolution.

Delacroix's political connections helped him secure permission to travel with French diplomats to Spain, Morocco, and Algeria in early 1832. What he witnessed in those places deeply affected his subsequent paintings. Overcome by the sights and sounds of the bazaars and the unique Arab-influenced architecture and culture, he sketched constantly. Like many Romantics, he came to associate Africa and the Middle East with the exotic and the sensual, if not the outright sexual, side of humanity. When he returned to France, he produced several canvases with "Oriental" themes. His visions of the Arab world are evident in two paintings, one entitled *The Lion Hunt* (1858 and 1861), which depicts mounted horsemen dressed in turbans and flowing garments attacking lions with swords and pikes in a riot of color and motion, and in the more subdued *Arabs Traveling* (1855).[30]

The above-mentioned artists have had a profound effect on the art world to the present. Romantic painters felt their duty was to reject the restrictions established by Classical traditions in favor of freedom and creativity. Moreover, the Romantics emphasized the individual and his need to truly express his feelings and discover the spiritual qualities within his soul.[31] The overt religiosity is most pronounced among the German painters. Whereas some Romantics, most notably the French, painted the exotic, the gruesome, and even the insane, they all elevated the landscape to great art. Beyond their experimentation with new themes, the Romantic painters also challenged traditional practices and techniques. They often painted outdoors. They also played with perspective and use of color. Romantic painters conveyed freedom and emotion that would only be brought to greater heights by those individuals associated with Romantic music.

Notes

1. Aidan Day, *Romanticism* (New York: Routledge, 1996), 54–55; William Vaughan, *Romanticism and Art* (New York: Thames and Hudson, 1994), 267.

2. David Blayney Brown, *Romanticism* (New York: Phaidon, 2001), 15, 45, 48, 127–128; Vaughan, *Romanticism and Art*, 132 and 136.

3. Brown, *Romanticism*, 197–198.

4. Ibid., 391–392; H. G. Schenk, *The Mind of the European Romantics* (Garden City, NY: Doubleday/Anchor, 1969), 39–40; Vaughan, *Romanticism and Art*, 100.

5. Brown, *Romanticism*, 71–72, 84–85, 120.

6. Ibid., 317.

7. Ibid., 42, 254–255, 283; Vaughan, *Romanticism and Art*, 263.

8. Brown, *Romanticism*, 161–162.

9. Morse Peckham, *The Birth of Romanticism, 1790–1815* (Greenwood, FL: Penkeville Publishing Co., 1986), 225–230, 318.

10. Vaughan, *Romanticism and Art*, 158–159, 163.

11. Brown, *Romanticism*, 19, 161; Maurice Cranston, *The Romantic Movement* (Cambridge, MA: Blackwell, 1994), 75–76; Peckham, *The Birth of Romanticism*, 231, 314–315; Vaughan, *Romanticism and Art*, 73.

12. Brown, *Romanticism*, 178–184.

13. Peckham, *The Birth of Romanticism*, 233.

14. Ibid., 311. Claude Monet was well-known for using this technique in his series paintings, such as haystacks and the façade of the Rouen Cathedral, among others.

15. Vaughan, *Romanticism and Art*, 201.

16. Brown, *Romanticism*, 184–185.

17. Ibid., 21–22; Vaughan, *Romanticism and Art*, 184–185, 207.

18. Constable and Wordsworth met through the auspices of their mutual patron Sir George Beaumont. See Peckham, *The Birth of Romanticism*, 233–235.

19. Ibid., 189.

20. Cranston, *The Romantic Movement*, 38; Peckham, *The Birth of Romanticism*, 189–190, 196; Vaughan, *Romanticism and Art*, 142–143.

21. Peckham, *The Birth of Romanticism*, 191–192.

22. Brown, *Romanticism*, 123.

23. Charles Sala, *Caspar David Friedrich and Romantic Painting* (Paris: Terrail, 1994), 139, 143, 148–151.

24. Vaughan, *Romanticism and Art*, 142.

25. Peckham, *The Birth of Romanticism*, 182–183; Brown, *Romanticism*, 135–136.

26. Brown, *Romanticism*, 24–25, 133, 136–137; Peckham, *The Birth of Romanticism*, 189; Vaughan, *Romanticism and Art*, 138–142.

27. Vaughan, *Romanticism and Art*, 233–234, 238–241.

28. Ibid., 248.

29. Brown, *Romanticism*, 4–5; Vaughan, *Romanticism and Art*, 249.

30. Brown, *Romanticism*, 348, 401.

31. Ibid., 10, 13.

CHAPTER 5

THE MOST ROMANTIC ART: MUSIC

Some discussions of Romanticism suggest that its essence can best be captured in music because it is the only art that is "immaterial," that is, it has no physical substance. Therefore, music is the best means to reach the Infinite (although many poets and painters would disagree with that assessment). This debate about music's special quality began with theoretical writings that defined Romanticism early in the 1800s, particularly E. T. A. Hoffmann's essays. He claimed the new music, with its emotional inclination, captured man's essential dilemma: the desire to be part of this world but also the wish to escape.[1]

Deciding when Romantic music flourished is as difficult as choosing the exact dates for the Age of Romanticism itself. Some historians argue that Romantic music should date from 1828, the year Schubert died, to 1883, the year Wagner died. Others suggest 1789 to 1914, the so-called long nineteenth century.[2] Rather than argue about specific dates, it is more important to understand what connects Romantic music to previous musical styles and what themes and characteristics help define it. Themes that pervade Romantic music reveal its connection to contemporary literature and painting, a characteristic which differentiated it from Classical music. Musicians incorporated an intensity of feeling in their compositions, and many alluded to escapism, especially to rural areas, because cities were overcrowded. Others chose to highlight nationalistic themes as a way to develop local pride.[3] These composers chose freedom of expression over the rules that overshadowed Classical music. The image of the isolated or misunderstood artist was associated with Romantic music as well. The composer must suffer, like a religious martyr, in order to reach beyond the everyday and reveal God's presence in nature through his works. The composer/musician becomes the means by which the universe becomes understandable to ordinary man even though the musician's special talent marginalizes him from society.[4]

Advocates of Romantic music claimed to reject Classical traditions, which seemed old-fashioned and predictable, whereas the new music embodied sensuality, freedom, and creativity. Yet, upon examining musical forms such as the sonata and the symphony, it becomes apparent that Romantic composers did not completely reject Classical models, but adapted them to allow for more personal expression. To do so, the Romantics expanded harmonic boundaries and forms that had been set by luminaries such as Wolfgang Amadeus Mozart (1756–1791).[5] They did so by breaking from the tradition of using only seven of the twelve keys in an octave on a piano and used all twelve, when possible, in order to give the music greater feeling and color. The use of the twelve-note (or chromatic) scale also allowed for easier changes in key. Composers could then write more complex works as well as use new instruments. Their music became identifiably Romantic because melody became more important than harmony.

What connected Classical and Romantic music? Instrumental music dominated the Classical style, and its structural basis was the sonata, a work in three movements and a coda. Depending on the number of instruments used in the performance of the sonata, it could be called a symphony, a concerto, a string quartet, sextet, or trio. Classical composers standardized the forms of instrumental music: the symphony, concerto, chamber music, and keyboard sonata. The Romantic composers, like their Classical predecessors, emphasized instrumental music. With no words to distract the audience, instrumental music conveyed pure feeling, so central to the Romantic perspective, and allowed for true flights of the imagination. These composers favored the symphony and the keyboard sonata; therefore, the music most associated with the Romantic era involves an orchestra or a solo instrument, usually the piano.

The development of Romantic orchestral music mirrored changes in the composition of the orchestra itself. In its basic form, an orchestra contained numerous instruments which when played simultaneously produced music with great feeling and texture. In the mid-eighteenth century, an orchestra consisted of about twenty-five instruments, mostly strings with a few winds and a keyboard. The orchestra Mozart wrote for was a little larger. But when Ludwig van Beethoven's (1770–1827) Ninth Symphony premiered in 1824, the orchestra consisted of sixty-one instruments and a chorus; the additional instruments were primarily reeds and horns. Within a decade, the average orchestra comprised seventy to eighty musicians, fifty of whom played strings. The orchestral sound changed not only because of the increased number of instruments but also because the quality of instrument manufacture improved, allowing for clearer and louder sounds as well as the expansion of harmonic sounds, giving the music more texture.[6] After Beethoven, the masters of nineteenth-century orchestral music include Schubert, Berlioz, Mendelssohn, Liszt, and Brahms.

The other important form of Romantic music involved solo instruments. The piano became most popular because it could be played in someone's home and in a concert hall. The instrument itself underwent structural improvements too, especially the development of the full iron frame which could handle the thicker strings. The latter created a sound with greater volume or sonority, that is, a full, deep, and rich sound.[7] Piano pieces ranged from short, sprightly dances to long, involved concertos, and solo works could display the performer's virtuosity. Many Romantic composers excelled as pianists, such as Schubert, Mendelssohn, Clara Wieck Schumann, Chopin, and Liszt.[8]

Romantic vocal music differs from Classical more noticeably than does instrumental music. Three forms reveal this difference: the *Lied* (art song), choral music, and opera. The *Lied* brought together music and poetry, which Romantic composers made longer and more involved than eighteenth-century examples. As story lines grew more complex, the singer and pianist had to express the contrasts and drama. In some cases, the piano was meant only as accompaniment to the singer, but in others, piano and singer were treated as equals. The most noted *Lieder* composers were Schubert, Robert Schumann, Clara Wieck Schumann, and Brahms.[9]

Romantics, such as Berlioz, Liszt, Rossini, and Verdi, also composed choral music, a form most often associated with the Roman Catholic Church, primarily high masses and requiems (funeral masses). Composers followed contemporary trends and wrote dramatic symphonies for orchestra and chorus based on biblical texts. However, Church officials often viewed such productions as too secular and nationalistic.[10]

Romantic composers also contributed to vocal music's most dramatic form, the opera. In the secular form of early opera, known as *opera seria*, the characters fulfilled their heroic destinies but always followed the behavioral standards of the day. The plots tended to be artificial and complex. The singers dominated the form with little overt drama, and the orchestra played in the background. By the 1720s, audiences demanded lighter and funnier story lines and more naturalistic dramas. Operatic reform in the eighteenth century came to be associated with Christoph Willibald Gluck (1714–1787) and W. A. Mozart. Romantic opera composers picked up from the eighteenth-century reforms the legacy of greater drama and sympathetic characters. They used the orchestra to "set the stage" by depicting a forest landscape or an approaching storm. The composers also created the continuous operatic act, which helped plot development. The growing tendency to realism in operas responded to nineteenth-century political issues, especially nationalism.[11]

Because of Italy's strong operatic tradition, it remained least affected by trends in Romantic music, whereas in France and Germany greater experimentation prevailed. France's grand opera dominated the middle of the nineteenth century with its great musical and dramatic scope, for example, Charles Gounod's (1818–1893) *Faust* (1859) and Georges Bizet's (1838–1875) *Carmen* (1874). German operas, especially those written by Richard Wagner (1813–1883), defined this form for the later Romantic era. Wagner advocated the *Gesamtkunstwerk* (the total work of art), by which he meant everything—the poetry/lyrics, set design, staging, dramatic action, and the music—fused to create the opera. His works, often based on mythology, are massive stage productions that highlight German nationalism. His most important legacy to subsequent composers was his emphasis on opera as great drama. Major composers of the Romantic opera include Gioacchino Rossetti, Giuseppe Verdi, Georges Bizet, Hector Berlioz, Carl Maria von Weber, and Richard Wagner.

Some of the nineteenth century's most memorable operas are Russian, including Mikhail Glinka's (1804–1857) *Ruslan and Lyudmila* (1842) and Modest Mussorgsky's (1839–1881) *Boris Godunov* (1872). These works, like those of the Russian masters of orchestral music and ballet, Nikolai Rimsky-Korsakov (1844–1908) and Piotr Ilyich Tchaikovsky (1840–1893), are caught up in the discussion of Romanticism and nationalism as it affected Russia of the nineteenth century. These works draw heavily on folk melodies and themes which give the music a distinctly Russian character. Yet, at the same time, Russian composers drew from western Europeans to create identifiably Romantic music. Arnold Whittal argues that "admiration of and stimulation by the major Romantic masters was a more crucial factor in the development of the best Russian composers than willingness to shackle their musical instincts in the abject service of texts."[12] This occurred in part because no formal music theory instruction was available in Russia until the founding of the Russian Musical Society in St. Petersburg in 1859.[13]

In the Romantic era, the sites of musical, especially vocal, performances expanded from salons and drawing rooms to concert halls and opera houses. The changes reflected the broadening of culture from the *ancien régime* society, dominated by the nobility, to the post-French Revolution era where the middle class became patrons of the arts. Vocal performances occurred in private homes where a pianist and singer entertained their audience with song cycles. The middle class also formed the audiences that gathered at the new public music venues.

Beethoven

Ludwig van Beethoven straddles the divide between Classical and Romantic music. He personally did not wish to be associated with the new musical style, but his compositions became the benchmarks by which later self-proclaimed Romantics measured themselves. From 1794 to 1801, Beethoven's compositions mirrored earlier traditions, especially the sentimental music of Carl Philipp Emanuel Bach (1714–1788). Nevertheless early in his career, Beethoven composed two important piano sonatas, Nos. 8 and 14, better known as the *Pathétique* (1791) and the *Moonlight Sonata* (1801), which reflect a Romantic tendency—individual expression.

Around 1801, Beethoven reportedly felt the need to do something different because he believed his previous compositions only reflected a style inherited from his musical predecessors.[14] The Third Symphony, *Eroica*, written in 1803 and 1804, evinced his new direction, which was marked by an expansion of form and harmonic vocabulary. First performed in April 1805, the audience was surprised by its length; it took fifty minutes to perform. (Mozart's longest symphony took about half that time.) The symphony explores the assertion of human will and follows a pattern from tragedy to hope. The musicians found the symphony difficult to perform, and the audience was uncertain about its quality. Nevertheless, this symphony inaugurated Beethoven's new musical style.

Another symphony, No. 6, *The Pastoral* (1808), clearly reveals Beethoven's connection to Romanticism. The inspiration came as he wandered in the woods near Vienna where the sights and sounds of nature gave him a special insight about himself. In the symphony, the orchestra not only recreates a thunderstorm but also a bubbling brook with chirping birds.[15] This symphony serves as an early example of program or illustrative music where the music virtually creates scenes for its listeners, one of Romanticism's important contributions to Western music.

After 1815, Beethoven wrote fewer works, but these later compositions have greater complexity.[16] The best known are the Mass in

D (*Missa solemnis* [1822]) and the Ninth Symphony (1824). Beethoven regarded the mass as his greatest work, and he followed the traditional pattern: the mass has five different sections. But unlike a Handel mass, where each part is a unique musical piece, Beethoven's mass is a planned unit. The premiere of the Ninth Symphony occurred in May 1824 at a concert which began with sections from the Mass in D. The symphony challenged the established practices associated with instrumental music. The eighteenth-century "standardized" symphony consisted of four sections: a fast opening, a slow movement, a minuet, and a fast finale. But Beethoven decided to write a symphony which also included a chorus and solo voices. During the premiere night, the audience reacted wildly, applauding and waving handkerchiefs, but Beethoven, being deaf, could not hear what was happening. One of the singers apparently got his attention and made him turn around so he could see the spectacle. The Romantics loved the Ninth Symphony because the music displays a supreme subjectivity; it is intimate, but it is also grand and brings about a feeling of the sublime in the listener.

The great Beethoven is known through his incomparable music, but the private man must be accessed through his correspondence. (See Primary Document 16.) He regarded himself as an artist, a gifted genius who created art as a legacy to future generations. One music historian referred to Beethoven as the tree trunk from which the branches of nineteenth-century music emerge.[17] Who were Beethoven's heirs?

Schubert

Although a gifted composer, Franz Schubert (1797–1828) lived almost entirely under Beethoven's all-too-large shadow. In 1808, the young Schubert won a scholarship to Vienna's Imperial Seminary where his musical talent emerged, and he began composing. With his song "*Gretchen am Spinnrad*" ("Gretchen at the Spinning Wheel" [1814]), Schubert enhanced the German art song, commonly referred to as the *Lied*. This song used poetry from Goethe's *Faust* (1808); when set to Schubert's melody, the listener could hear the spinning wheel turn.

By 1820, Schubert had begun to compose a series of string quartets which, along with his songs, became the focal point of musical evenings in many Viennese upper-middle-class households. Schubert and Johann Michael Vogl (1768–1840), a well-known baritone, often performed together. The popularity of these intimate pieces, *Lieder*, piano, and chamber music, reflected the shifts in cultural norms associated with the early decades of the nineteenth century. Whereas Beethoven had cultivated aristocratic patrons, Schubert associated with the middle class.

Schubert grew ill in 1822 as he was working on what has come to be known as the *Unfinished Symphony*. It is so called because it has only two complete movements rather than the standard four. It is a restless and tragic composition, using strings and then oboe and clarinet to carry the haunting melody. Some regard Schubert's *Unfinished* as the first truly Romantic symphony.[18] The remainder of his life, Schubert battled illness and poverty, at times he had no residence and periodically moved in with sympathetic friends. Nevertheless he composed masterpieces. The year 1828 witnessed his greatest compositions, including his Ninth Symphony (*Great Symphony in C Major*), which reflected very creative use of brass instruments, String Quartet in D minor (*Death and the Maiden*), and a song cycle entitled *Winterreise* (*A Winter's Journey*).

Schubert wrote an incredible amount of music during his short life. He conceptualized an entire work in his head before putting a note on paper, which helps explain the speed at which he composed. His legacy consists of nine symphonies, seventeen operas, twenty-three piano sonatas, numerous string quartets, and over six hundred songs. While Schubert did not create the *Lied* format, it remains chiefly associated with him. Like Beethoven, Schubert has been categorized as both a Classical and Romantic composer because while his works follow Classical structural standards, their emotionality is truly Romantic.[19]

Berlioz

Hector Berlioz's (1803–1869) orchestral and choral works stand as unique entities that carry on the Romantic tradition of music as great art, filled with emotion. Unlike his fellow composers, Berlioz did not play piano, and he taught himself harmony by reading about it. Berlioz lived in Paris, writing music and singing professionally, in the mid-1820s. His first major composition, *Symphonie fantastique* (1830), allegedly was finished as gunfire sounded near Berlioz's quarters signaling the July Revolution that dethroned King Charles X. Regardless of whether this happened, the symphony was first performed in December 1830. In this symphony and others, Berlioz experimented with Classical rules about musical harmony. The *Symphonie fantastique* stands as a milestone in modern music because, with it, Berlioz perfected the art of program music. Simply put, this music tells a story through the expressing mood and emotion.

Its subtitle, "Episodes in the Life of An Artist," hints at Berlioz's innovations concerning the symphonic form. Instead of an abstract piece, the story depicts a young artist, disappointed in love, who tries to kill himself. Rather than die, the hero falls into deep sleep and has incredible dreams. The symphony's first three movements reveal the beloved as a recurring theme that haunts him. The artist and his lady are separated; he finds her at a masked ball. Later still, he is in a meadow listening to folk melodies and she reappears, but by now he is convinced of her unfaithfulness. By the fourth movement, he has killed her and is executed for the crime. Finally, in the fifth, he attends a witches' sabbath, and, in the midst of an orgy, she reappears to join in. Her theme by now has lost its dignity and reserve and has become a trivial tune.

Berlioz suffered from financial problems in the 1840s, despite having composed some of his best works in the previous decade, and he turned to writing music reviews and also conducting. He also toured Europe, spreading the word about the new music with its dramatic feeling. Through his work with various orchestras, Berlioz made another critical contribution to Romantic and subsequent music. He liked to conduct large orchestras, and his intuitive sense of combining instruments and adding new ones to the orchestra, which broke with traditional practices, heralded a new direction for music. In 1844, he wrote *Treatise on Instrumentation*, which became not only the first textbook dedicated to orchestration but also introduced the notion of expressiveness to music.

Chopin

Frédéric Chopin (1810–1849) is regarded as the greatest composer of solo piano music. He began composing at age six, a year before he started piano lessons. Chopin spent childhood summers at the country estates of family friends where he became acquainted with folk music when he attended village festivals. These experiences developed a lifelong connection to Polish folk music. When he was sixteen, Chopin began his studies in harmony and composition at the Warsaw Conservatory of Music. He then traveled to Vienna to broaden his knowledge of contemporary music. Political turmoil in the Austrian Empire forced him to move to Paris where he encountered a large Polish exile community. While living there, he composed music to honor his homeland, which included *mazurkas* (folk dances) and *polonaises* (marches). His support for Polish nationalism was so important to him that his last concert was dedicated to Polish refugees and soil from his homeland was strewn on his grave in Paris.

While living in Paris, Chopin met many of the new talents, including Liszt and Mendelssohn, and began teaching and composing. He earned enough from his piano students that he did not have to perform in concert halls—something he truly disliked. His reputation spread throughout the city, and he was often invited to perform in private residences. In 1836, Chopin met writer George Sand (see Chapter 3), and within two years, they became lovers. Their nine-year relationship was critical for Chopin as Sand provided him with the love and care he needed. At Sand's estate in central France during the summers, Chopin enjoyed rest, relaxation, and good air; but he also found inspiration. During this period, he composed twenty-four preludes, the *Polonaise in C Minor*, and the *Ballade in F Major*, among other works.

Chopin, like no musician before him, understood the piano as an instrument that could be used to perform Romanticism's expressive pieces. His music, graceful if at times melancholy, often included many concise pieces that explored one idea. He did not pound the instrument, as had been Beethoven's tendency; rather, Chopin's restrained style has been referred to as magical or poetic.

The Schumanns

Robert Schumann (1810–1856) and Clara Wieck Schumann (1819–1896) contributed jointly to Romantic music. Although his family wanted him to study law, Schumann was determined to become a concert pianist. By 1832, he had published his first major piano pieces, *Abegg Variations* (1830) and *Butterflies* (1829–1831), but he began to experience physical difficulties with his right hand. Because he could not attain greatness as a concert pianist, he turned his energies to composing and writing music criticism, founding a music journal in 1834. He fell in love with piano prodigy Clara Wieck shortly thereafter and composed a work specifically for her, *Arabesque in C Major*, Opus 18 (1838–1839). He also traveled to Vienna, where he discovered Schubert's *Lieder* and became an enthusiast of this form.

In 1840, he composed many *Lieder* that are still performed today, including *A Poet's Love*, which uses the poetry of Heinrich Heine (1797–1856) to tell a typically Romantic tale. In the song, a poet falls ecstatically in love only to be rejected and isolated, and as a result, he wishes to die. Unlike some *Lieder* composers, Schumann did not allow the vocal portion to overwhelm the instrumental. He often wrote *Lieder* in which, after the vocal part concluded, the piano continued, the music itself evoking further emotion.

Clara Wieck, now married to Schumann, encouraged him to expand his compositions beyond piano music and *Lieder* into symphony and other orchestral works. From there, he moved on to chamber music and then wrote what he termed a "secular oratorio" called *Paradise and the Peri* (1843). He also composed one opera and other choral music. In these formats, however, Schumann was not particularly successful.

Clara Wieck Schumann noted that the day she married Robert was the happiest of her life. Both Robert and Clara composed *Lieder* during their early years of marriage. Robert's compositions had wide variety, and he experimented with putting together unexpected text and music. Clara's songs emphasized the piano and tended to be direct and sincere. They chose widely different poems to set to music: Robert sought out works full of metaphor, while Clara picked poems that expressed concerns about religion and family life.

The Schumanns contributed to Romantic music in three ways: (1) Robert expanded on the *Lieder* tradition established by Schubert by intentionally seeking out complicated texts and juxtaposing them with interesting melodies which teased out emotional content. (2) Robert's critical essays brought to the public's attention the new music and those composers actively creating it. (3) Clara performed and promoted the new music in concerts across Europe.

Liszt

Born in Hungary, Franz Liszt (1811–1886) serves as Romanticism's equivalent of a present-day rock star: tall and good-looking, he charmed his audiences whenever he performed. His success was not simply due to his appearance; he undoubtedly was the greatest pianist of all time, and he has a central place in the Age of Romanticism. Not only did he compose many noteworthy symphonies and piano works, he also played and familiarized his audiences with the music of Beethoven, Schubert, and Robert Schumann.

Liszt debuted in Paris in 1824, and he became a sensation. In the late 1820s, he embarked upon a concert tour to France and Switzerland that left him exhausted. His father's death shortly after that tour ended and a failed love affair left Liszt depressed; he did not touch the piano for a year. In 1830, Liszt acquired a renewed focus, which led to him to compose *Revolutionary Symphony* (1830), commemorating the July Revolution.

Subsequently, Liszt met three musicians who greatly influenced him. The first was Hector Berlioz whose *Symphonie fantastique* introduced Liszt to the monumental in music. He learned orchestration from Berlioz and the concept of putting emotions into compositions. Second, the violin virtuoso Nicolo Paganini (1782–1840) provided Liszt with the model of technique and showmanship that Liszt adapted to his piano performances. Third, Frédéric Chopin showed Liszt that piano performances could be poetic and subdued and did not have to be overly dramatic.

By 1834, Liszt had become a mature piano composer and his musical efforts focused on transcribing the orchestral music of Beethoven and others for piano performance. In the late 1830s, Liszt resumed touring Europe and performing. He visited Hungary for the first time since he had left as a young boy, and experienced Gypsy music that inspired him to write the *Hungarian Rhapsodies* (1846–1885).

In 1848, Liszt moved to Weimar and became the official court musician. The eleven years he spent there were his most active as a composer. He wrote two symphonies based on great literary works: Goethe's *Faust* and Dante's *Divine Comedy*. Liszt abandoned the three-to-five movement symphonies and concertos in favor of one sweeping movement. He made an important contribution to music at this point by developing the symphonic poem, a one-movement work with great freedom and flexibility. Artistic and personal differences with the Weimar court led Liszt to move to Rome. There he became interested in church music and eventually composed his *St. Elizabeth* oratorio (1857–1862). In 1869, Liszt was invited to return to Weimar to perform. For the remainder of his life, he traveled between Rome, Weimar, and Budapest, taking on music students.

Liszt's legacy has many facets: he invented the symphonic poem; he was the first to present piano recitals in which he used no sheet music; and he captured the full potential of the piano. At many concerts, he had two pianos on stage, and when the first went out of tune because of his enthusiastic playing, he would turn to the second and continue. He also set the standards for modern conducting. He did not act like a living metronome as earlier conductors had; he got the orchestra to play with feeling and fluidity. In true Romantic style, Liszt's compositions provide stories of heroes and their successes and failures. He also wrote deeply religious works, which provoked reflection on the divine.

Synthesizing Classical and Romantic Tendencies

The presence of those individuals who cultivated the new Romantic style did not mean the end of Classical music. Two major composers contemporary to the Romantics must be mentioned: Felix Mendelssohn and Johannes Brahms. Both embodied Classical and Romantic tendencies in their compositions. Felix Mendelssohn (1809–1847) frequented Berlin social circles consisting of philosophers, actors, artists, and musicians. At twelve, he met Goethe and the two established a strong friendship. Mendelssohn's well-rounded education exposed him to Classical music, and the works of J. S. Bach, Handel, and Mozart stood out as his favorites. He also read Romantic literature, which he apparently did not enjoy.[20]

He visited Paris in 1831 where he met Chopin and Liszt. Around this time he wrote his most identifiably Romantic music. Like his Romantic contemporaries, Mendelssohn used literary works for inspiration, including Shakespeare's *A Midsummer Night's Dream* and Goethe's *Faust*. Landscapes also inspired him, as is evident in his Symphony No. 4, entitled *The Italian* (1833). Mendelssohn loved the logic of music so, even though thematically his works paralleled those of the Romantics, his style in some cases was more reserved and reflected Classical forms. Mendelssohn, like Liszt, also helped raise the standards of orchestral performance and the art of conducting. He promoted the careers of fellow musicians such as Robert and Clara Wieck Schumann and made the Leipzig Conservatory a respected European music center.

Johannes Brahms (1833–1897), a conservator of the eighteenth-century Classical tradition, embarked on his first concert tour in 1853, with a violinist friend. He met Liszt in Weimar and the Schumanns in Düsseldorf. Shortly after Robert's breakdown in 1854, Brahms returned to help Clara. He developed a deep attachment to her, and she remained his musical mentor throughout their lives. In the late 1850s, he premiered his first orchestral works and completed his first piano concerto.

In 1868, Brahms decided to settle permanently in Vienna, reinvigorating the city's great musical tradition. He did continue concert tours, but focused on composing. In a work that brought him fame, *The German Requiem* (1868), he explores the themes of death, mourning, and consolation found in biblical texts. Reflecting both Classical and Romantic styles, the *Requiem* maintains a Classical form but stretches the melodic and harmonic boundaries. Shortly thereafter, he published *Hungarian Dances*, light dance melodies influenced by Gypsy music. He was acknowledged as a German national composer during the euphoria of the Franco-Prussian War (1870–1871) and its aftermath.

He did not complete his first symphony until he was forty-three. He took his time because, feeling that he carried the legacies of the great Classical masters on his shoulders, he wanted to create a perfect piece of music. Within the decades of the 1870s and 1880s, Brahms produced four masterful symphonies. In addition to his great orchestral works, Brahms must also be recognized for his concertos for solo instruments and his *Lieder*. His *Wiegenlied* (1868), better known as *Brahms' Lullaby*, was written to celebrate the birth of a friend's child and remains popular to this day. Although Brahms personally remained distant from Romanticism, he should be regarded as a composer straddling the two musical traditions. He wrote music that has Classicism's technical perfection, but its themes are emotion laden.[21]

The Romantic musical tradition continued the Classical preference for instrumental music, especially the great orchestral symphonies and piano concertos. The more intimate forms of music, such as the short piano pieces, string quartets, and *Lieder* also formed an important part of the Romantic repertoire. The music itself broke from the balanced formalism of the Classical tradition and sought, through its new combinations of tones, to "paint pictures." It tried to project feeling and patriotism. Opera grew in style and grandeur and its format came to be standardized through the works of the nineteenth-century composers. The musicians wanted their works to directly affect the emotions of their audiences. The troubles of the external world were to be forgotten as people allowed emotions to soar as they listened to the music. Through this experience, each person could seek an interior calm or spirituality, that search for the Infinite so characteristic of Romantic aspirations.

Notes

1. Friedrich Blume, *Classic and Romantic Music: A Comprehensive Survey*, trans. by M. D. Herter Norton (New York: W. W. Norton, 1970), 95–99, 112–113, 117; Morse Peckham, *The Birth of Romanticism, 1790–1815* (Greenwood, FL: Penkeville Publishing Co., 1986), 95–96.

2. Rey Longyear, *Nineteenth Century Romanticism in Music*, 2nd ed. (Englewood Cliffs, NJ: Prentice-Hall Inc., 1973), 1–2.

3. Ibid., 3–6; Harold C. Schonberg, *The Lives of the Great Composers*, 3rd ed. (New York: W. W. Norton, 1997), 144.

4. Blume, *Classic and Romantic Music*, 112, 116; Peckham, *The Birth of Romanticism*, 88.

5. Blume, *Classic and Romantic Music*, 107–108, 115, 129–130; Longyear, *Nineteenth Century Romanticism in Music*, 2; Schonberg, *The Lives of the Great Composers*, 141–142.

6. Barbara Russano Hanning, *Concise History of Western Music* (New York: W. W. Norton, 1998), 380–381.

7. Adolphus Babcock of Boston produced the first full iron frame for an upright piano in 1828. It was cast as one piece. See Max Wade-Matthews and Wendy Thompson, *The Encyclopedia of Music* (London: Hermes House, 2002), 228–229.

8. Blume, *Classic and Romantic Music*, 147–148.

9. Longyear, *Nineteenth Century Romanticism in Music*, 56.

10. Hanning, *Concise History of Western Music*, 431.

11. Longyear, *Nineteenth Century Romanticism in Music*, 53–54.

12. Arnold Whittall, *Romantic Music: A Concise History from Schubert to Sibelius* (New York: Thames and Hudson, 1987), 134.

13. Ibid., 131. See pp. 129–141 for the discussion of Romantic opera in Russia.

14. Peckham, *The Birth of Romanticism*, 143–144. Many sources describe the lives and works of composers. When not cited with another source, detailed information came from Schonberg, *The Lives of the Great Composers*, 3rd ed., passim.

15. David Blayney Brown, *Romanticism* (New York: Phaidon Press, 2001), 132–133.

16. Longyear, *Nineteenth Century Romanticism in Music*, 78.

17. Ibid., 82–83.

18. Hanning, *Concise History of Western Music*, 376.

19. Longyear, *Nineteenth Century Romanticism in Music*, 97.

20. Whittall, *Romantic Music*, 34.

21. Arnold Whittall suggests that Brahms actually synthesized three musical traditions: Baroque counterpoint, Classical symphonism, and Romantic expressive immediacy. It was not so much that Brahms rejected the Romantic tendencies in music, but that he had such a curiosity about all kinds of music that he incorporated them in his works. Whittall, *Romantic Music*, 164–165.

CHAPTER 6

ROMANTIC LEGACIES: NATIONALISM AND ENVIRONMENTALISM

Many people may debate the certainty of Isaiah Berlin's statement: Romanticism "seems to me to be the greatest single shift in the consciousness of the West that has occurred, and all the other shifts which have occurred in the course of the nineteenth and twentieth centuries appear to me in comparison less important and at any rate deeply influenced by it."[1] It definitely challenged the certainties of Enlightenment thought and its rational basis for problem solving and endorsed a cult of feeling, which characterizes Romantic literature, painting, and music. Romanticism has also left a vast and complex cultural legacy to the modern world. The artists of that era responded to the world around them in many ways. Some rejected the present and yearned for an idealized past. Others viewed their artistic gift as a means to explore the issues of the present and a way to bring insight to the rest of humanity. Some championed individual freedom of expression. The challenges unleashed by the Romantics have survived well into the twenty-first century. Romantics explored universal versus particular experiences and the individual and community. Those themes intertwine with two of Romanticism's important legacies: nationalism and environmentalism.

Nationalism

"Nationalism is the desire among people who believe they share a common ancestry and a common destiny to live under their own government on land sacred to their history."[2] This definition leads in two directions with respect to Romanticism's relationship to nationalism and its subsequent history. One traces the consolidation of a national cultural identity among various European peoples. The other follows the development of the concept of political community and its manifestation in the nation-state.

Most discussions of Romanticism and nationalism begin with German philosopher Johann Gottfried von Herder (1744–1803). He resented how French-influenced Classicism dominated the intellectual and artistic high culture of Europe. Herder's fears originated with his notion about a people's identity and relationship to their culture. According to him, each people (*Volk*) developed a unique culture (*Kultur*), which depended on a common historical past and a particular place. This fact naturally divided all humanity into identifiable nations. Within these cultural nations, the artist's task was to embrace societal norms and appropriately present aesthetic and moral values in his works, which reflected the nation's collectivity. The French cultural hegemony hindered this natural process, especially for the German lands.[3] Herder's vision accepts that each nation develops unique standards. Herder, a deeply religious man, believed that the divine presence within the human community will lead to cooperation among peoples. The vehicle whereby this will take place is the nation-state.[4]

Herder believed that for the nation-state to succeed, it had to be tied to the cultural nation, and it is here that the Romantics join the discussion. They act as purveyors of cultural values through such efforts as developing a uniform literary language. They also study the past to evoke a common history, whether real or imagined, in their works.[5] The Romantic artists' efforts at validating national cultural identity began in Germany and Great Britain and then moved to France, Italy, and Russia in the 1820s.

Their quest to find a sense of identity in the present by studying the past initially involved folk songs and tales passed down orally over the generations. The process of collecting folktales, carried out by the Grimm brothers (Jacob Grimm [1785–1863] and Wilhelm Grimm [1786–1859]), in German-speaking lands, served as a model which other folklorists followed. The Romantics also explored linguistic traditions and local religious practices. They bridged the gap between elite culture and that of the ordinary people by discovering a national identity based on these folk traditions. As a result, they defined their community based on language, customs, religion, and common geography, often referred to as cultural nationalism.

The Romantics' interest in identifying various cultural communities influenced the proliferation of folk costumes and festivals. Many thought the peasant traditions had greater spiritual value than those associated with the modern urban world. Thus folk arts became a focus of study as well as a means of identifying a people's national origins. The unique craftsmanship associated with folk art separated it aesthetically from the uniformity of machine-made products.

The question of political nationalism is more problematic but it has been a crucial force of the past two centuries. The discussion of political nationalism starts with German philosopher, Johann Gott-lieb Fichte (1762–1814). His *Addresses to the German Nation* (1808), given in 1807 and 1808 after Napoleon's victories over Austria and Prussia, appealed to the Germans' sense of national identity, which needed invigoration after the recent humiliation. (See Primary Documents 4.)[6]

The works of the Romantic nationalist historians such as Jules Michelet (1798–1874) play a role here as well. His discussion of the French Revolution, for example, the storming of the Bastille, reveals the ordinary Frenchman as a hero battling the repressive forces of the Bourbon monarchy. Michelet was the first of many prominent nineteenth-century national historians, including Prussian Heinrich von Treitschke (1834–1896). His history of Germany reveals a pro-nounced bias in favor of Prussia's might and how it should lead Germany on the path to national greatness.[7]

The Romantics' quest for cultural uniqueness contributed to the evolution and consolidation of modern nationalism. They worked within the collective identity of their cultural nation, producing works that had particular spiritual essence because of that connection. The artists, as individuals, embodied the collective whole through their works. Their intellectual efforts at defining their cultures in opposi-tion to others, however, transformed into a mutating political concept, which remains active in today's world. Although modern nationalism derived from the legacy of eighteenth-century Western political revolu-tions, it has spread in many forms around the world. Many argue that the process of globalization today makes the nation-state obsolete, yet nation-alism remains a vital force.

Nature and the Environment

Romantic writers, artists, and musicians often turned to nature as inspiration or refuge. Beyond this spiritual connection, the Romantic love of nature reflects the general rejection of the city and the complications associated with urban life. While remaining essen-tially forward-thinking in outlook, they regretted that the rational-ist tradition had reduced nature to a mechanism. The authenticity of nature's beauty, untouched by humankind's corrupt hands, could inspire fear or awe. When the Romantics could escape to remote locations, the peace and solitude facilitated their search for the Infinite. They, through their unique artistic gifts, could show their contemporaries the divine in nature and help them overcome disenchantment with the modern world.[8]

The Romantic veneration of nature, in part, related to a phenomenon that began in the middle of the eighteenth century. Between 1750 and 1770, Europeans began to ascend the Alps, which not only provided a physical challenge but also aided scientific efforts by amateur geologists and botanists, such as Goethe. (See Primary Document 17.) The mountains that John Keats ascended were not that high, but they were nevertheless inspiring. The sport of mountain climbing was born, and by 1865, the summits of the Alps' tallest mountains were reached. The popularity of mountain climbing continued into the twentieth century. Well after the Alps had been conquered, other mountain chains drew adventurers. Sir Edmund Hillary's conquest of Mt. Everest in 1953 stands as the most daring and dramatic event in the history of mountain climbing. Of course, Everest and K2, the Himalayas' tallest peaks, still attract adventurers today. Although they may use oxygen and technological devices to help them, modern climbers are still carrying the seeds of Romanticism with them.

While climbers ascended to the mountaintops, in the valleys Romantic authors rented chalets and took from mountain views inspiration for their works. A famous product of a summer at a Swiss alpine retreat is Mary Shelley's *Frankenstein*. Countless poems and short stories describe not only the grandeur of the mountains with their pristine glaciers but also the dangers that can be associated with such remote places. While inspirational nature can be synonymous with mountainous regions, the Romantics' love for nature could also be found in the flatland, too. Beethoven's walks in the Vienna woods inspired some of his greatest music. A ramble in a meadow covered with wildflowers could also promote raptures, as evident in William Wordsworth's poetry.

The Romantics' focus on nature helped generate the modern environmental movement. Many grappled with the issue of the individual confronting a world changing because of industrial and political forces. Some Romantics not only preached a return to nature, but wished to see the spread of industrialization stopped or even reversed. More practical people recognized that this idea was impossible and suggested controlled industrial expansion in order to preserve as much nature as possible, a perspective often called Conservationism.[9]

The modern world's advance against the natural environment emerges in the poetry of John Clare (1793–1864). (See Primary Document 18.) From impoverished circumstances and with little education, as a young man he wrote poems evoking local Northamptonshire scenes. He called attention to the enclosure of common and waste lands in the name of rationalized agriculture which upset the local natural balance. Clare acutely responded to the destruction of rural environments.[10] Clare represents the ecological side of environmental discourse that perceives humans as part of nature, neither above it nor able to control it. His poetic style, ungrammatical and unpunctuated, was intentional. He made up words to simulate bird sounds and wanted to capture the essence of plant and animal life in all its varieties. These devices were intended to reveal his organic connection with nature and trigger in his readers an appreciation of the inherent dangers associated with tampering with the natural world.[11]

Like Clare, William Wordsworth represents "an individualist environmental awareness" that serves as a lasting legacy of Romanticism. It has been argued that Clare had a truly environmental concern for nature, whereas Wordsworth's appreciation was much more intellectual. For Wordsworth, in a similar vein to the views of Caspar David Friedrich, nature in its pristine wildness is a means to truly experience the sublime.[12] Dorothy Wordsworth, on the other hand, sees the beauty of the landscape, yet also appreciates rural people and their culture. (See Primary Document 19.)

Wordsworth's poetry alludes to the beauties of nature in Romantic terms and how it serves as a source of artistic creativity. However, his *A Guide to the Lakes* ties him directly to the environmental tradition. The 1835 version included a preface, "Directions and Information for the Tourist." More than a travel guide, Wordsworth believed it could engage the tourists' minds as they wandered about the Lake District.[13] Wordsworth did not advocate getting rid of the tourists, rather, he wanted to educate them so that their actions would not destroy the environment. He described the Lake District as a national treasure that everyone should enjoy. That kind of language inspired various individuals and led to the founding of the National Trust in 1895, the guardian of Britain's coastlines, countryside, and historic places.[14]

Appreciating and protecting nature took many directions in the twentieth century. The two world wars and the social and economic turmoil of the 1920s and 1930s overwhelmed or misdirected the environmental legacy. It remained to the 1950s and beyond for the environmental discussion to regain its voice. At that time, it took on a global perspective. But beyond conservation and preservation of natural spaces, the new direction turned ecological.[15] The critical event that brought this issue to public awareness occurred with the publication of Rachel Carson's *Silent Spring* (1962). A quotation from Keats appeared in the book's front matter: "The sedge is wither'd from the lake, / And no birds sing."[16] Indeed, the revolution begun by Rachel Carson had spiritual roots in Romanticism. Her insistence on the critical need to ban DDT brought the environment and its fragility into public discussion.

The various directions modern-day environmentalism has taken in the Western world involve personal and political strands. The former includes those people dedicated to organic farming, using natural fertilizers and living a life not overburdened by the products of an industrial world. The rural commune experiments and farms begun in the 1960s and 1970s reflect this commitment. The political direction led to the formation of Green political parties, which involve two kinds of activists: environmentalists and ecologists. The former expresses a practical response to industrialization and its problematic legacies. They wish to clean up or stop pollution and adopt a reasoned approach to future development to hinder its threat to the natural world. The ecologists are more drastic: they cry out on behalf of the finiteness of the world's natural resources. Some want large-scale industrial growth stopped and, in its place, small enterprises, friendlier to the environment, created to carry out the world's manufacturing needs.[17]

The Romantics certainly would have favored these contemporary environmental efforts. They sought individual and artistic inspiration from nature, and most wanted its pristine beauty protected. Their suspicion about the spread of industrialization, while based on personal and aesthetic considerations, led to a focus on its environmental aftereffects and ways to respond.

Conclusion

This discussion reveals how concerns associated with the Romantics remain intrinsic to the modern world—in this case, nationalism and environmentalism. The Romantics railed against the changes their society underwent as a result of rationalist legacies, political upheaval, technological advances, and social realignments. The pace of modernization, as it is called today, seemed overwhelming.

In trying to answer the great questions about human existence, Romantic artists turned to nature for inspiration. Their aesthetic sensibilities allowed them to use their imaginations to create works of art, but these were not ends in themselves. They served rather as physical reminders of the artist's imagination and its critical role for the rest of humanity. According to Romantic thought, without an active imagination a person could never understand or really appreciate his surroundings. The imagination, this mysterious force found in human consciousness, served as the critical link between the individual self and the divine. The imagination facilitated the artist's ability to respond to physical surroundings and from that to comprehend the great truths in life. What is truth? What is beauty? What does it mean to be human? The artist's task is to discover answers to these questions and convey personal insights to others. This, in turn, would excite within the reader, viewer, or listener a self-transformation or a voyage of discovery. The questions the Romantics confronted are still very much with us today, and they can be thanked for their answers for what it means to be human in a certain place and time and how to confront the stresses the world places upon everyone.

Notes

1. Isaiah Berlin, *The Roots of Romanticism* (Princeton, NJ: Princeton University Press, 1999), 1–2.

2. Robert H. Wiebe, *Who We Are: A History of Popular Nationalism* (Princeton, NJ: Princeton University Press, 2002), 5.

3. David Calleo, *Rethinking Europe's Future* (Princeton, NJ: Princeton University Press, 2001), 54–55; Charles Larmore, *The Romantic Legacy* (New York: Columbia University Press, 1996), 36–37.

4. Calleo, *Rethinking Europe's Future*, 53, 55–56.

5. Ibid., 50–51; Patrick Geary, *The Myth of Nations: The Medieval Origins of Europe* (Princeton, NJ: Princeton University Press, 2002), 16–17.

6. Lloyd Kramer, *Nationalism, 1775–1865* (New York: Simon and Schuster, Macmillan, Twayne Publishers, 1998), 39.

7. Ibid., 55–56.

8. Robert J. Richards, "The Erotic Authority of Nature: Science, Art, and the Female during Goethe's Italian Journey," in *The Moral Authority of Nature*, ed. Lorraine Daston and Fernando Vidal (Chicago: University of Chicago Press, 2004), 128; Helmut Schneider, "Nature," in *The Cambridge History of Literary Criticism Vol. 5 Romanticism*, ed. Marshall Brown (New York: Cambridge University Press, 2000), 96–97.

9. Colin Riordan, "Green Ideas in Germany: A Historical Survey," in *Green Thought in German Culture* (Cardiff: University of Wales Press, 1997), 4–5; Donald Worster, *Nature's Economy: A History of Ecological Ideas* (New York: Cambridge University Press, 1985), 81–92.

10. James McKusick, "'A language that is ever green': The Ecological Vision of John Clare," *University of Toronto Quarterly* 61 no. 2 (Winter 1991): 226–231.

11. Riordan, "Green Ideas," 45; Tony Pinkney, "Romantic Ecology," in *A Companion to Romanticism*, ed. Duncan Wu (Malden, MA: Blackwell, 2001), 414; McKusick, "'A language that is ever green' ...," 240–245.

12. Jonathan Bate, *Romantic Ecology: Wordsworth and the Environmental Tradition* (New York: Routledge, 1991), 39–40; Timothy Morton, "Environmentalism," in *Romanticism: An Oxford Guide*, ed. Nicholas Roe (New York: Oxford, 2005), 700; Worster, *Nature's Economy*, 83.

13. Bate, *Romantic Ecology*, 41–47; Pinkney, "Romantic Ecology," 417.

14. Bate, *Romantic Ecology*, 48.

15. Riordan, "Green Ideas," 8.

16. As quoted in the front matter of Rachel Carson, *Silent Spring Twenty-fifth Anniversary Edition* (Boston: Houghton-Mifflin, 1987), n.p.

17. Riordan, "Green Ideas," 4.

11

My bones are pierced in me in the night season & my sinews take no rest

My skin is black upon me & my bones are burned with heat

The triumphing of the wicked is short, the joy of the hypocrite is but for a moment

Satan himself is transformed into an Angel of Light & his Ministers into Ministers of Righteousness

With Dreams upon my bed thou scarest me & affrightest me with Visions

Why do you persecute me as God & are not satisfied with my flesh. Oh that my words were printed in a Book that they were graven with an iron pen & lead in the rock for ever For I know that my Redeemer liveth & that he shall stand in the latter days upon the Earth & after my skin destroy thou This body yet in my flesh shall I see God whom I shall see for Myself and mine eyes shall behold & not Another tho consumed be my wrought Image

Who opposeth & exalteth himself above all that is called God or is Worshipped

WBlake invent & sculp

William Blake, "With Dreams upon my bed" from *The Book of Job*. Museum of Art, Rhode Island School of Design. Gift of Mrs. Jane W. Bradley in memory of Charles Bradley

Henry Fuseli, *The Nightmare* (1781). Founders Society Purchase with funds from Mr. and Mrs. Bert L. Smokler and Mr. and Mrs. Lawrence A. Fleischman. Photograph © 1954 The Detroit Institute of Arts

Caspar David Friedrich, *The Polar Sea* [*Das Eismeer*] (1823–1824). Photo: Elke Walford. *Bildarchiv Preussischer Kulturbesitz*/Art Resource, NY

Philipp Otto Runge, *The Hülsenbeck Children* (1805–1806). Photo: Elke Walford. *Bildarchiv Preussischer Kulturbesitz/* Art Resource, NY

Ferdinand-Victor-Eugène Delacroix, *Arabs Traveling* [*Arabes en voyage*] (1855). Museum of Art, Rhode Island School of Design. Museum Appropriation Fund

Biographies

Ludwig van Beethoven (1770–1827)

Born in Bonn, Beethoven was the oldest of three surviving sons of Johann and Maria van Beethoven. His father, a musician at the Archbishop of Cologne's court, wanted his son to become a musical prodigy, but Beethoven's talents did not blossom until Christian Neefe (1748–1798), the court organist, became his instructor and arranged for the young Beethoven to study with Mozart in Vienna in 1787. He remained only a short while in Vienna because family issues called him back to Bonn, where he joined his father as a court musician and also instructed wealthy piano students. A noble patron eventually helped Beethoven return to Vienna to study with Haydn in the early 1790s. Known as a skilled pianist, Beethoven had a reputation for improvising. He played with so much feeling that he could evoke tears from his audience. He gave his first public concert in Vienna in 1795 and he subsequently made concert tours of the eastern European capitals. By 1796, he had published several piano pieces that challenged Classical music's boundaries of balance and moderation.

He recognized he was going deaf in 1800, and his musical style began to change. Suffering from depression and contemplating suicide, nevertheless he went on to write some of his most famous works, including *Eroica*, the Third Symphony (1803), which took twice as long to perform as the traditional symphony. His first opera, *Fidelio* (1805), with its theme the brotherhood of man, was only performed twice, greatly disappointing him. He turned to composing only instrumental music, and in 1808, the Fifth and the Sixth Symphonies premiered. After Beethoven began receiving annual support from wealthy patrons, he devoted himself exclusively to composing. After E. T. A. Hoffmann's favorable commentary about the Fifth Symphony, published in 1810, Beethoven's music got wider exposure, and his international fame grew. By 1818, his deafness made him withdraw from society although he continued to compose. The music he wrote from 1815 to 1827 is noted for its diversity. He completed his greatest religious work, *Missa solemnis*, dedicated to Archduke Rudolph, in 1822 and two years later the masterpiece Ninth Symphony.

Beethoven lived a rather isolated life. He allegedly fell in love with several women, all of whom were unattainable because of their marital or social status. In 1815, he took over guardianship of his nephew Karl, but the uncle and nephew had a difficult relationship culminating in Karl's attempted suicide in 1826. Beethoven, ill at the time, sketched out what would have been his Tenth Symphony. He died in late March 1827 and ten thousand people watched his funeral procession.

Beethoven was the first composer to write music that reflected his personality. Initially, he composed what he thought patrons would want to hear (and pay for), but then he declared he would compose according to his inspiration and imagination. He paved the way for Romantic composers to succeed him by creating music full of emotion, subjectivity, and individuality.

Hector Berlioz (1803–1869)

Born near Grenoble in the French Alps, into a physician's family, Louis-Hector Berlioz grew up in well-to-do circumstances. He had little formal training in music as a child and appeared to have worked out harmony on his own by reading about it. He took flute and guitar lessons as a youngster, becoming quite proficient at the latter. His father sent him to Paris in 1821 to study medicine, but the young man found medical studies repellent. He frequently attended performances at the Paris Opera and decided to turn to a musical career. He began studies privately and then eventually enrolled in the Paris Conservatoire. His decision did not please his parents and led to an estrangement.

Between 1827 and 1830, Berlioz lived in Paris, writing music and singing professionally in order to pay the bills. He was exposed to the music of Beethoven and Carl Maria von Weber (1786–1826), the German composer known for his Romantic and nationalist inspired opera *Der Freischütz* (The Free Shooter), and became a convert to the idea that music should be dramatic. Berlioz also discovered Shakespeare and Goethe at this time. In 1827, he attended a performance of *Hamlet*, where he was smitten with Irish actress Harriet Smithson, who played Ophelia, with whom all of Paris had fallen in love.

Meanwhile in 1830, Berlioz won the prestigious Prix de Rome, which did reconcile him with his family. In this year, his first major composition *Symphonie fantastique* was performed. He could not capitalize on its enthusiastic reception in Paris, because his prize required that he go to Rome. He languished in Italy, away from all the stimulation that had been his world in Paris. Nevertheless, he did meet some of music's leading composers while there, including Mikhail Glinka (1804–1857) and Felix Mendelssohn (1809–1847).

Personal attachments brought him back to Paris in 1832, so he lost the stipend associated with his prize. Through a series of coincidences he reconnected with Harriet Smithson. They eventually married one year later, but theirs was not a happy marriage and they separated after a few years. He took up with opera singer, Marie Recio, who remained his mistress until Harriet died from alcoholism in 1854. He and Marie married and ostensibly the two were quite happy, until her death eight years later.

He produced many noteworthy works during the 1830s, among others the symphony *Harold en Italie* (*Harold in Italy* [1834]), inspired by Byron's *Childe Harold's Pilgrimage*. Later in the decade he wrote *Roméo et Juliette* (*Romeo and Juliet* [1839]), a choral symphony, dedicated to the great violinist Paganini. As part of the Parisian music scene, Berlioz knew he had to prove himself by writing a great opera, which resulted in *Benvenuto Cellini* (1838). It was not well-received at its premiere and that affected Berlioz's reputation in France, whereas the rest of Europe seemed to be taken by him.

From the 1840s on, Berlioz due to financial concerns undertook a series of exhausting tours across Europe. He was promoting the new dramatic style of music and showing conductors around the Continent how to deal with the new music. He is referred to as the first virtuoso conductor. His last tour in 1867 found him in Russia, where he introduced young composers there, such as Modest Mussorgsky (1839–1881), to the new style of conducting. The orchestras themselves had to be taught to play the new music, a task which Berlioz undertook with great success. He returned to Paris in ill health and subsequently experienced the tragic death of his son, a sea captain, who died of yellow fever, while in Cuba. Berlioz himself died in Paris in 1869.

William Blake (1757–1827)

Born in London, Blake grew up in moderate circumstances. His father sold hosiery, gloves, and related accessories. Despite having no

formal schooling, he wanted to be an artist and at ten entered drawing school, where he remained for four years. He then apprenticed
to an engraver at fourteen, and during the next seven years, he studied engravings of great Renaissance paintings and the statues at
Westminster Abbey.

He entered the Royal Academy at twenty-one earning a living
as a journeyman engraver, illustrating novels and magazines. By
1782, he had married, and within a year, *Poetical Sketches* (1783)
appeared, containing poems written during his teens. Over the next
two years, Blake experienced personal tragedy and business failure.
He claimed a vision of his brother, who had died from consumption
in 1787, provided insight about "illuminated printing," a technique
Blake used to produce his subsequent books. He took a copper plate
and "painted" his design with a special liquid. After an acid bath, a
relief with the text and illustration emerged, which would be printed
on paper. As a final touch, the spaces were water-colored. Because of
this involved process, editions of Blake's books appeared in small
numbers.

His first works in this style *There is No Natural Religion* (unfinished) and *All Religions are One* (c. 1788) explored Blake's philosophy. He criticized John Locke's idea that the human mind is a blank
slate that life experiences fill in. Blake opposed the rational and
materialist philosophy and instead stressed the superiority of imagination over sense perception. He believed that only through imagination could man understand God.

Between 1789 and 1794, Blake produced many works, including
the poetry collections *Songs of Innocence* (1789) and *Songs of Experience* (1794). He addressed issues such as acquisitive materialistic society and sexual awakening in some of the works. The simplicity of his
language foreshadowed other Romantic poets' styles. Blake responded
to the turmoil of the 1780s and 1790s through social commentary.
His *French Revolution* (c. 1791) praises the defeat of monarchy and
the rise of democracy; *America* (1793) explores the theme of revolution in general terms; and, *The Marriage of Heaven and Hell* (1793)
criticizes organized religion and the state as oppressive forces.

Blake's poetry was little known in his day, but during the 1790s
his reputation as an engraver grew, and he received many commis-
sions. Between 1803 and 1820, financial hardship forced him to
devote his energies to engraving. He wrote two great epic poems,
however, including *Jerusalem* (1804), which explored man's fall and
redemption and was illustrated with one hundred plates. In *Jerusalem*, Blake called for the awakening of human senses, so mankind
could perceive the spiritual around him.

In his last years, Blake cultivated a circle of young artists, who discussed art with him. One of his students helped get Blake a commission to illustrate the *Book of Job* (1826). Blake's last engravings are regarded as his most technically proficient and most beautiful. Blake died in London, working on his last commission, engravings for an edition of Dante's *Divine Comedy.*

George Gordon, Lord Byron (1788–1824)

George Gordon was born in London with a club foot. His mother brought him to Scotland as an infant to escape his father, who had squandered her fortune. Mother and son lived in meager circumstances until he inherited the title Lord Byron and they returned to England to live at Newstead Abbey. While attending boarding school, his lameness caused him to be ridiculed, and in response to such experiences, he befriended younger boys, who had also been subjected to harassment. His attachments were alleged to be romantic and reflective of his ambivalent sexuality. In 1805, he entered Cambridge University, where he gambled, drank, and incurred debts. He privately published his first volume of poetry *Fugitive Pieces* (1806). A bad review of his work led to a sarcastic commentary, *English Bards and Scotch Reviewers* (1809), which won him attention in literary circles.

In 1809, Byron took his seat in the House of Lords and within months he embarked with a friend on a grand tour, which included Portugal, Spain, Gibraltar, Malta, and Greece. Impressed with Greece and its people, who seemed warm and friendly compared with the cold, reserved English, he began *Childe Harold's Pilgrimage* during this trip. He returned to England in mid-1811. About this time, the first two parts of *Childe Harold's Pilgrimage*, a discussion of a young man's thoughts on rejecting the "wild life," made him famous. Drawn into London society, he had several liaisons with older aristocratic women. He then married Anne Isabella Milbanke (1792–1860) in early 1815, but after their daughter's birth at year's end, Anne left him. He departed England never to return.

He lived near Geneva in mid-1816, together with the Shelleys and Mary Shelley's step-sister Claire Clairmont (1789–1879), who had become his mistress while he was still in England. He continued *Childe Harold's Pilgrimage* and other works and, in the fall, moved to Venice and began an affair with his landlord's wife. Other romantic adventures led to *Beppo* (1818), a sarcastic poem contrasting English and Italian manners and morals. In late 1818, Newstead

Abbey was sold to clear up Byron's debts and provide him an annual income.

Unhappy, although financially secure, he became fat and lazy, but a new love revived him and led to his most productive period. He wrote *Don Juan* (1819–1824), an epic poem which transforms the legendary ladies' man into an unsophisticated youth, who enjoys the wild life, but still remains a rational critic of the crazy world around him. Byron moved to Pisa in 1821, where his lover and her family and the Shelleys lived. In early 1823, Byron was contacted by the London Greek Committee concerning the Greek war against the Turks. He joined Greek forces at Missolonghi in December, where he got involved in plans to attack a Turkish-held fort. He fell ill in February and died in April.

Samuel Taylor Coleridge (1772–1834)

The youngest of a large family, Coleridge spent his childhood with books. His father, a vicar and schoolteacher, expected Coleridge to become a clergyman, and when he entered Cambridge in 1791, he began studies for the Anglican priesthood. His attraction to Unitarianism and his philosophical studies turned him from this career. Financial difficulties led Coleridge to enlist in the army, where he served five months. He returned to Cambridge but then left for a summer walking tour of Wales in July 1794, never to resume university studies.

That year he met Robert Southey (1774–1843) with whom he became friends. Their musings about the French Revolution and society's shortcomings fostered the idea of a utopian community, a pantisocracy, an equal government by all. They wanted twelve families to immigrate to North America to form such a community. As part of the plan, Southey and Coleridge married sisters, Edith and Sara Fricker, but their dream never materialized. Coleridge, meanwhile, was left in an unhappy marriage.

He embarked on a full-time career as a writer, publishing two poetry volumes in 1796 and 1797. Interested in politics, he founded a journal, *The Watchman*, but published only ten issues in 1796. In 1797, the Coleridges settled near William Wordsworth and his sister Dorothy. The two men began a collaboration which resulted in the *Lyrical Ballads* (1798). Coleridge's "The Rime of the Ancient Mariner" and other poems published in this collection revealed Wordsworth's influence on Coleridge's style.

A stipend from a wealthy friend allowed Coleridge, accompanied by the Wordsworths, to travel to Germany for the winter of

1798–1799. Coleridge attended lectures at Göttingen University, where his exposure to German Romanticism led him to introduce English audiences to its ideas. Upon his return to England, he settled his family near the Lake District and developed an attachment to Sara Hutchinson, Wordsworth's future sister-in-law. Plagued by ill health since his early twenties, he had used opium for ten years and by 1803 he probably was an addict. In 1804, he traveled to Malta, where he hoped the warmer climate would rejuvenate him. He returned to England after travels in Italy and subsequently obtained a legal separation from his wife in 1806. His friend Robert Southey stepped in to care for Coleridge's former wife and children.

Coleridge and Wordsworth grew estranged, in part because of Coleridge's attachment to Sara. Embittered, Coleridge moved to London, where he felt totally abandoned yet also achieved fame. His continued opium use ruined his health, and he often failed to appear for lectures. Meanwhile concerned friends sent money to support him. In 1816, Coleridge moved in with Dr. James Gillman, who regulated Coleridge's opium intake, allowing him to renew his writing. Within a year, *Biographia Literaria (Biographical Sketches of My Literary Life and Opinions* [1817]) appeared, which combined autobiography, philosophical musings, and literary criticism. He continued to write mostly prose in his later years and died in 1834.

Johann Wolfgang von Goethe (1749–1832)

Goethe grew up in a middle-class family in Frankfurt and had an ostensibly happy childhood. His father was a lawyer and his mother was the daughter of a public official. His university career began in Leipzig, where he studied law as well as writing, art appreciation, and architecture. He wrote plays and short stories. An illness forced him to return home, but he later resumed studies at the University of Strasbourg. There he developed a deep interest in German cultural traditions. He wrote *Götz von Berlichingen* (1773), which focuses on a medieval knight and his battle to pursue his right to think and act as he wishes. Influenced by Shakespeare's style, this play broke with the Classical dramatic traditions of time, place, and action.

In 1771, Goethe joined his father's law practice but continued writing. *The Sorrows of Young Werther* (1774), where the hero commits suicide because of an unhappy love affair, brought him literary fame. Shortly after the book's appearance, Goethe took a political post with the Duke of Saxe-Weimar, which he held for eleven years. He enjoyed life in the provincial capital of Weimar, where he associated with members of high society and fell in love with a married woman. Between 1786 and 1788, he traveled in Italy, and upon his return to Weimar, he withdrew from his ministerial position to become a full-time writer. His play *Torquato Tasso* (1790) explores the agony of a poet whose creativity or genius makes him unfit for everyday life.

In the 1790s, Goethe met Friedrich Schiller (1759–1805), who shared his belief that the arts made a man a better person and citizen. It was at this time that the Romantics of the Jena Circle sought out Goethe; he seemed flattered by their attention, but remained skeptical of their literary goals. He and Schiller collaborated on dramas, a literary journal, and managing the local royal theater. When Schiller died in 1805, Goethe felt that half of himself had also perished.

Although Goethe's fame as a writer, dramatist, and amateur scientist grew, he withdrew from public contact. His most famous drama, *Faust,* appeared in two parts, in 1808 and 1832. *Faust* tells the tale of a disillusioned scholar, who, in return for selling his soul to the devil, will learn all the mysteries of the universe. This *Sehnsucht* (yearning) for some thing or someone becomes a recurring theme in Romantic literature. In Goethe's version, Faust is redeemed by angels because he has learned that the meaning of life involves service to humanity and work for the greater good of all.

Throughout his later years, Goethe remained an active writer and completed his memoirs *Dichtung und Wahrheit* (*Poetry and Truth*) between 1811 and 1822. Although he was not a very religious man, Goethe did feel God's handiwork could be seen in nature. Like the Romantics, he believed each person had a spark of the divine in himself, which gave everyone the power to reach his potential. Goethe died in Weimar at age eighty-two.

E. T. A. Hoffmann (1776–1822)

Born in Königsberg, Prussia, Ernst Theodor Wilhelm Hoffmann, who changed his second middle name to Amadeus to honor Mozart, had many careers: writer, composer, conductor, painter, and civil servant. The family expected Hoffmann to follow the profession of his father, a lawyer. Although he studied law at the University of Königsberg, Hoffmann's first love remained the arts. He entered the Prussian civil service in 1795 and served in various small towns, but in 1802, he offended several superiors and was transferred to a remote location in Prussian-controlled Poland. Through connections, Hoffmann eventually got posted to Warsaw, where he became involved with a musical society and a local theatrical company. He established an orchestra, conducted it, and also wrote his first musical selections. The French army's occupation of Warsaw in 1806 put his government job at risk; when he refused to swear an oath of allegiance to the French, he was forced to leave.

After scrounging for work in Berlin for two years, he moved to Bamberg in 1808 and became the local orchestra's conductor. Although that job only lasted nine months, it did serve as a watershed, as he subsequently turned almost exclusively to writing. Although he still gave music lessons on the side, after 1809, his stories began appearing in magazines. He also composed music, including an opera.

Hoffmann suffered from ill health between 1812 and 1814 while living in Dresden, where he worked as a conductor and lived through another French occupation. He wrote some of his most famous short stories then including "The Golden Flower Pot" and "The Sand Man." He lost the job in Dresden, but a friend helped him secure another in Berlin. He accepted a post with the Prussian Supreme Court and was recognized as a fair judge. His new job left him plenty of time to write and to associate with the Berlin literary set. In 1816, he organized a collection of his short stories and witnessed the successful production of his opera *Undine*. In his last years, he suffered from bouts of paralysis, yet he continued to write. A conflict with a superior led Hoffmann to write a satire in which the main character parodied the official with whom Hoffmann had had trouble. He had to undergo a disciplinary hearing, but could not attend the proceedings because of his deteriorating health. He died June 25, 1822, in Berlin.

Victor Hugo (1802–1885)

Born the third son of a father who served as an officer in Napoleon's army, Victor Hugo grew up primarily in Paris. He began university studies in the law faculty in Paris, but was not a devoted student. His fascination with Vicomte de Chateaubriand (1768–1848) and his writings led Hugo to decide to become a writer. In 1819, he founded a literary review in which he not only published his poetry, but also that of Alphonse Lamartine (1790–1869). In 1822, he married Adèle Foucher with whom he had five children, four of which survived infancy. He published his first volume of poetry that year. The following year he founded another journal, *Muse Française* (1823–1824) and collaborated with many well-known Romantics such as Byron and Sir Walter Scott. From the mid-1820s on, Hugo published several volumes of poetry, where Romantic themes such as love and terror appear. The volume *Les Orientales* (1829) explored the Greek War of Independence.

The "Preface" to his drama *Cromwell* (1827) aligned Hugo with Romanticism. In this lengthy document, he supported the new Romantic literary ideas and even though he couched his language carefully, the ideas he espoused offended many. They disliked his dismissal of the Classical rules about drama, the so-called three unities of time, place, and action, and his notion that a play could contain comedy and tragedy. It was at the production of his play *Hernani* in February 1830 that fights broke out between those who supported the old versus the new style of drama.

The next year, Hugo published *The Hunchback of Notre Dame* (1831), which brought him fame. His poetry from this time is filled with emotion and reactions to current events. His drama *Le Roi s'amuse* (*The King Is Amused* [1832]), which takes place in Renaissance France and discusses the loves of King Francis I, was banned after one performance. Censors believed that the play, even though set in earlier times, criticized the current monarchy. Not a particularly good work, it has lived on because it inspired the libretto for Verdi's *Rigoletto* (1851).

In the middle of the 1840s, he endured several personal tragedies and also formed a close friendship with King Louis-Philippe's family. Despite this attachment, during the aftermath of the Revolution of 1848, he supported Louis-Napoleon's presidency of the republic. But after Louis-Napoleon named himself Emperor in 1851, Hugo left France. From his exile, he composed *Les Châtiments* (1853), which contained political poems attacking Louis-Napoleon. Hugo grew bored with the restricted nature of political poetry and published in 1856 what is called his purest book of poetry *Les Contemplations*, which was heavily influenced by his interest in the surreal.

In 1862, after seventeen years' work, his masterpiece *Les Misérables* appeared, which was immensely popular in France and was quickly translated into many languages. After France's defeat in the Franco-Prussian War, Hugo returned to Paris. He got involved in national politics and held a seat in the National Assembly. He died in Paris in 1885, a national hero, and two million people joined his funeral procession.

John Keats (1795–1821)

Little is known of John Keats's early life. He was the eldest child of five born to a livery-stable manager and his wife in London. After his father's death in 1804, his mother quickly remarried, which proved to be a mistake. In relatively quick succession, Keats's mother and grandmother died. John was removed from school and apprenticed to an apothecary/surgeon. Although Keats learned the trade, he wrote poetry too.

In 1815, Keats moved to London, where he worked as a junior house surgeon at a couple of hospitals, but his real commitment remained to poetry. He published his first poems in 1816 and also earned an apothecary license, but he abandoned medicine to take up his dream of becoming a poet. Virtually penniless, he made friends among the London literary circles and published *Poems* (1817). At this time, Keats embarked on a four-month tour of various rural English sites. The solitude he enjoyed allowed him to compose his lengthy poem *Endymion* (1818), in which he explored man's search for ideal love.

In the summer of 1818, he undertook a walking tour of the Lake District and Scotland but returned showing signs of the tuberculosis which had killed his mother and would soon kill his brother. Around this time, Keats met Fanny Brawne, and their initial attachment grew into love, but because of his failing health and precarious finances, they never did marry. In 1819, Keats's most productive year, "The Eve of St. Agnes," "*La belle dame sans merci*," "Ode on a Grecian Urn," "Ode to a Nightingale," and "Ode on Melancholy" appeared.

Early in 1820, Keats suffered a massive lung hemorrhage, an unmistakable sign of tuberculosis. He worked intermittently and published an 1820 volume of poems, which were well received. An advance from his publisher gave Keats the money for a trip to Italy to improve his health. He settled in Rome under the care of a resident Scottish doctor. Keats wrote many letters from Rome but no poetry. He died there February 23, 1821, and was buried in the Protestant Cemetery.

Alessandro Manzoni (1785–1873)

Born in Milan, Manzoni spent his early years in the care of strangers, separated from his father Don Pietro and his mother Guilia, the daughter of Cesare Beccaria. The twenty-seven year difference between his parents led to Giulia separating from her husband when Manzoni was only seven. The boy attended several religious boarding schools and although he apparently did not enjoy any of them he was a good student. He spent summer vacations at a family estate near Lake Como and those interludes developed in him a sincere love of that region.

After study at the University of Pavia, he moved to Paris in 1820 to take up residence with his mother, whose lover had just died. Manzoni was exposed to liberal circles at that time as his mother associated with the salon of Madame de Condorcet. He flirted with a Voltaire-inspired skepticism. His early poetry was inspired by Vincenzo Monti (1754–1828) and reflected Classical style. He married a Calvinist, Henriette-Louise Blondel, in 1808. After the birth of their daughter, the question of her baptism arose and after some deliberation Manzoni decided to have her baptized Catholic. By early 1810, Henriette had converted to Catholicism and they were re-married according to Catholic rite. His return to the Catholic Church is often credited with contributing to the Romantic turn that his poetry then took.

In 1810, Manzoni, his wife, child, and mother moved to Italy and settled in Milan, where he embarked on a full-fledged literary career. His initial works were religious poems, published as "The Sacred Hymns" (1815), which highlighted the church's feast days. The finest of them "Pentecost" appeared in 1822. His prose explored religion, "Observations on Catholic Ethics" (1819) and political matters, such as "March 1821," dedicated to Piedmont's revolution of 1821. The poem which brought Manzoni initial fame was "The Napoleonic Ode" (1822), written to commemorate Napoleon's death in 1821. Goethe heralded it as one of the best poems written about that event and it remains one of the most popular nineteenth-century Italian poems. His tragedies *The Count of Carmangnola* (1820) and *Adelchi* (1822), while not that well-received in Italy, were attempts to break Italian drama from the restraints of the Classical unities.

Manzoni began work on *I Promessi Sposi* (*The Betrothed*) in 1820. He realized that in a historical novel he could combine his chief passions: Italian history and religion. Its publication brought him fame at home and abroad as it fit well with the current European enthusiasm for historical novels made popular by Sir Walter Scott's *Waverley* and subsequent works. After the novel appeared, Manzoni committed himself to a linguistic movement known as the "Tuscanizing School." Its adherents wished to make the Tuscan dialect the official Italian literary language. He began intense linguistic study and then rewrote his novel in Tuscan. The new and improved *The Betrothed* appeared in 1840.

The remainder of his life was spent quietly. Henriette had died in 1833 and Manzoni remarried apparently happily. He outlived his second wife and seven of his nine children. He died in Milan on May 22, 1873, shortly after the death of his favorite son.

Aleksandr Sergeyevich Pushkin (1799–1837)

Born into an old *boyar* (noble) family, Pushkin grew up in a Moscow household that immersed itself in French culture. His early exposure to Russian traditions came from his maternal grandmother and his old nurse, a former serf. Like many great writers, Pushkin read widely as a child and began writing poetry as a teenager. He attended a prestigious preparatory school near St. Petersburg, which provided him with the best education available in Russia at that time. His first major poem, *Ruslan and Ludmila* (1820), originated from verses begun during his student days.

He took a political post in St. Petersburg in 1817 and initially led a carefree life. He joined several literary clubs and in one of them he met young Russians disgruntled with the tsarist government, some even participating in the Decembrist Uprising in 1825. Pushkin's poetry took inspiration from the reformist ideas of his friends and even though it was circulated in manuscript form, tsarist authorities discovered it. He was then banished from the capital in mid-1820 under the guise of being awarded another post in the southern part of the empire.

Exiled initially to the Ukraine, he relocated to the Caucasus Mountains and eventually to the Crimea. These locales provided inspiration for a series of Romantic poems referred to collectively as the "Southern Cycle." These poems along with *Ruslan and Ludmila* solidified his status as the leading Russian poet of the 1820s. During his initial years of exile, Pushkin associated with local notables, and got involved with drinking, gambling, and philandering. When he offended a local governor, he was relocated to a family estate near Pskov in 1824 and placed under house arrest. There he immersed himself in Russian history and learned folk songs from the peasants. His poetry, initially inspired by western European styles, took on a decided Russian identity. His noted poems included "The Gypsies" (1824), "The Bridegroom" (1825), and "Count Nulin" (1827). At this time, he began his play *Boris Godunov* (1830), in which he discusses the age-old question of order and authority, more specifically the interaction between the tsar and nobles and the Russian people. The play is lauded because it not only develops a historical plot, but also a psychological theme.

Tsar Nicholas I (ruled 1825–1855) allowed Pushkin to return to St. Petersburg in late 1826. Several of Pushkin's friends had been implicated in the Decembrist Uprising and some had been executed. Its failure led him to conclude that reform in Russia would have to come from the tsar in order to be successful. Although no longer in exile, Pushkin was constantly under the secret police's surveillance and he could neither publish nor travel without official permission. Nevertheless, between 1829 and 1836, he produced some of his greatest works including the dramas *The Covetous Knight* (1836), *Mozart and Salieri* (1831), *The Stone Guest* (1838), and *Feast in the Time of the Plague* (1832), short tales, literary criticism, and sketches. He also completed his great verse novel *Yevgeny Onegin* (1833), which was the first Russian novel to explore contemporary society.

After deciding to settle down, he spent several years looking for an appropriate wife. He eventually married the beautiful Natalya Goncharova in 1831 and the couple settled near St. Petersburg. Pushkin resumed a government post and was eventually promoted. Financial burdens acquired because of his father's and brother's indebtedness left Pushkin under much stress. His requests to resign from his post so he could relocate to the countryside and concentrate on his writing were denied. He wrote intermittently and finally completed *The Captain's Daughter* (1836), based on the eighteenth-century Pugachev Rebellion. He died as the result of a duel in January 1837, defending his wife's honor. Tsarist authorities wished to prevent a massive demonstration at his funeral so they held it in a small church with admission by ticket only. He was buried next to his mother at a monastery near Pskov.

Jean-Jacques Rousseau (1712–1778)

Born in Geneva, Rousseau lost his mother as a newborn and his watchmaker father worked sporadically, leaving the boy emotionally and financially impoverished. At ten, he moved in with his mother's relatives, who unsuccessfully apprenticed him to a notary and later to an engraver. At sixteen, he left Geneva, a penniless wanderer. Befriended by Madame de Warens of Savoy (1699–1768), he lived at her estate, and the two became lovers. There Rousseau learned manners, studied music, read philosophy and theology, and gained skills that later allowed him to enter polite society. For thirteen years, she found him various jobs, including work as a gentleman's secretary and as a music teacher.

In Paris at age thirty, he introduced his "discovery," a new kind of musical notation, which he expected would lead to fame and fortune. He met Denis Diderot and eventually wrote articles about music for the *Encyclopédie*. He served as secretary to the French ambassador to Venice in 1743–1744, but the abuse of power he witnessed there led him to develop a negative opinion about government. In 1745, he met Thérèse LaVasseur, a chambermaid, who became his lifelong companion and mother of his children. Rousseau gave all five of the children to orphanages because he felt he could not afford to raise them.

He gained fame with the publication of *A Discourse on the Sciences and Arts* (1750), wherein he stated that man in his natural state is good, but the arts and sciences have corrupted him. This theme continued in *A Discourse on the Origins of Inequality* (1753), which traces how the social order civilization imposes on man creates inequality based on property ownership. Rousseau's subsequent writings explored how man could return to equality.

His three major works appeared in the early 1760s, beginning with *Julie, or The New Eloise* (1761). The novel criticized superficial education and the unhappiness caused by social conventions in a plot that centered on the tragic love between a woman and a man below her social station. *Émile* (1762) explored Rousseau's ideas about the proper way to educate a young man and, in Book Five, a girl "Sophie." *Social Contract* (1762) suggested that mankind could achieve freedom by forming civil societies through a social contract. Man surrenders his individual will to a general will, which creates a state with just laws that work for the common good.

These works brought further fame, but religious and political authorities criticized *Émile* and the *Social Contract*, and, under threat of arrest, Rousseau fled the country, initially settling in Switzerland and later moving to Britain. He secretly returned to France in 1767. He began to write his autobiography, *Confessions* (1781–1788). The last few years of his life, he spent as a paranoid outcast and died at an estate outside Paris. Initially buried there, in 1794, his remains were moved to the Pantheon, located in the heart of Paris. This apotheosis occurred because Jacobin leaders of the radical phase of the French Revolution had adopted Rousseau's notion of the general will for their political ends and as an intellectual forbearer of the revolution, his remains needed to be honored appropriately.

Franz Schubert (1797–1828)

The relatively short life of Schubert reads like that of many Romantic-era artists. He had an extraordinary talent, but his dissolute lifestyle contributed to an early death. Born in Vienna into a schoolmaster's family, his father taught Schubert and his siblings to play instruments. Schubert himself excelled at piano, organ, and violin and performed along with his father and two brothers as a string quartet. In 1808, he won a scholarship to attend the Vienna Imperial Seminary, a prestigious private school. In addition to studying music and singing in the choir, he formed friendships with several well-connected young men, who would later help him financially.

Between 1814 and 1817, he taught at his father's school where he was a mediocre instructor. Rather than concentrate on teaching his pupils, he devoted himself to composing, which he did at night. He had a lifelong love of poetry and he set many well-known poems to music. This affinity for poetry allowed Schubert to capture the spirit of the poem through his music. Schubert's major contribution to Romantic music was the *Lied* or the German art song. In 1815, he composed one hundred fifty *Lieder*, many based on Goethe's poetry.

Schubert left his father's home because he decided to concentrate on writing music. He met Johann Michael Vogl (1768–1840), a popular singer, who became a frequent performer of Schubert's works. He wrote many songs during 1817 and also seven piano sonatas which reflected Beethoven's influence. The first public performance of Schubert's work occurred in the spring of 1818. Later that year, he spent five months at the estate of Hungarian nobleman Count Esterhazy, where Schubert taught the count's children music and had free time to compose. He then returned to Vienna and devoted himself entirely to his music. His extreme poverty forced him to move constantly, living with a series of friends. In 1820, he expended a great deal of effort writing two operas, neither of which was successful. Meanwhile, Schubert became frustrated at his marginal status.

By 1823, Schubert had contracted syphilis. Nevertheless, he composed the two movements of his famous *Unfinished Symphony*, and some sonatas. He also developed what became known as the song cycle, several songs linked together by a common theme. Schubert composed major works in the last year of his life, including the *Symphony in C Major* and the *Mass in E Flat*. His noted song cycle from this year was the *Winterreise* (*A Winter's Journey*). In March 1828, the Viennese Music Association organized a concert devoted only to

Schubert's music. This successful event was the only taste of fame Schubert experienced during his lifetime. He died on November 19, 1828, after three days of delirium. He was buried in the Währing Cemetery, near Beethoven.

Mary Wollstonecraft Godwin Shelley (1797–1851)

The only daughter of Mary Wollstonecraft and William Godwin, Mary grew up badgered by her stepmother Mary Jane Clairmont and home-schooled by her father. Mary read widely and in 1808 published a poem in a children's book. Well aware of her mother's intellectual legacy and knowing that her birth caused her mother's early death, she may have suffered psychologically.

Percy Bysshe Shelley met Mary in 1812, when he visited her father. Two years later, they "eloped" to France, leaving behind Shelley's pregnant wife and Mary's angry father. Mary gave birth to a premature girl, who quickly died. Her second child was born in early 1816. Shortly thereafter, Shelley, Mary, the baby, and her stepsister Claire, now Lord Byron's mistress, traveled to Switzerland, and Mary began work on *Frankenstein* (1818). The entourage returned to England, where shortly thereafter both Mary's half-sister Fanny Imlay (1794–1816) and Shelley's wife Harriet Westbrook (1795–1816) committed suicide. Shelley and Mary got married at year's end, and the following spring, another daughter was born. *Frankenstein: Or the Modern Prometheus* appeared anonymously in January 1818. Two months later, the Shelleys relocated to Italy and settled near Pisa. Unfortunately, both their young children died during this time. Meanwhile, Mary received word from England about her book's positive reviews.

In late 1819, Mary gave birth to her only child to survive infancy, Percy Florence Shelley (1819–1889). She continued to write. After Shelley's death by drowning in July 1822, Mary had Shelley's body cremated and the ashes buried in the Protestant Cemetery in Rome. She remained in Italy until mid-1823. After her return to England, she began to edit Shelley's poems, but when an 1824 volume appeared, her father-in-law Sir Timothy Shelley (1753–1844) threatened to cut off his meager support for her son, unless she stopped further publication—which she did. Sir Timothy's mean-spiritedness came from his inability to understand or appreciate his genius son and his literary works. In the early 1840s, she secured Sir Timothy's permission to publish some poems, but he still forbade the publication of a biography of Shelley.

Throughout her life, Mary wrote novels, journal articles, and book reviews to support herself and her son. She also received several marriage proposals, but refused them out of loyalty to Shelley. She eventually published Shelley's poetry and prose after his father's death and included her annotations to the poems. Mary died in London from a brain tumor at age fifty-three.

Percy Bysshe Shelley (1792–1822)

The eldest son of an aristocratic family, Shelley rebelled against its conventions, which destined him to inherit great landed estates and a seat in Parliament. Shelley attended Eton from 1804 to 1810, where he began writing poetry. Three factors influenced Shelley's perspective: his Classical education, the older generation of Romantic authors, and the radical political reformers of his day. He and other younger British Romantics shared a fascination with Ancient Greece which led to a desire to aid contemporary Greeks in throwing off the yoke of their Turkish overlords. He attended Oxford but was expelled after only two semesters because he and another student wrote the pamphlet "The Necessity of Atheism" (1811). Family connections could have gotten him reinstated, but to do so he would have had to declare himself a Christian, and he refused. His father then cut him off financially.

Shelley endured two years of poverty, yet he married Harriet Westbrook in August 1811, and the couple traveled in Ireland and England, circulating radical political pamphlets. He published *Queen Mab* in 1813; a long poem, it attacks what Shelley felt were past and present social evils including war, the power and authority of church and state, the restricted institution of marriage, and eating meat. Philosopher William Godwin (1756–1836), whom Shelley had met in 1812, strongly influenced his thinking. Shelley declared himself in love with Godwin's daughter Mary and the two ran off to the Continent in July 1814. Later that year, Shelley's grandfather died and his will provided Shelley an income.

In the summer of 1816, Shelley, along with Mary and her stepsister Claire Clairmont, moved to Lake Geneva to spend time with Lord Byron. That memorable summer, Shelley wrote poetry, while Mary began *Frankenstein*. After the Shelley party returned to England in September, his wife Harriet committed suicide by drowning, and he then married Mary in late December.

Shelley liked to challenge established values and as a result his narrative poem *Laon and Cythera* (1817) was quickly removed from public sale because of its discussion of incest and attacks against religion. Moreover, it depicted a peaceful national political revolution brutally suppressed by the power of church and state. Shelley reworked the poem and renamed it *The Revolt of Islam* (1818). His poetic commentary on the fleeting nature of fame and fortune, "Ozymandias," appeared in 1818 as well.

Early that year, due to health and financial concerns, Shelley moved his extended family to Italy and eventually settled on the Tuscan coast. Whereas poems written in England contained political or social commentary, in Italy, he turned to a more aesthetic approach. He could not change the world but maybe his poems could transmit his views about art and life. At this time, he composed *Prometheus Unbound: A Lyrical Drama* (1820), an elaborate story that explains the triumph of good over evil. His poem "Epipsychidion" (1821), which he wrote in honor of a young Italian woman with whom he formed an intense friendship, has been called the greatest poem in English about love.

In the summer of 1822, Shelley drowned along with a sailing companion after their boat was caught in a storm and apparently capsized. Mary spent the remainder of her life collecting and editing Shelley's works. She persisted at this task even though his father prevented her from publishing them during his lifetime.

Madame de Staël (1766–1817)

Anne-Louise Germaine Necker, better known at Madame de Staël, was born in Paris to Swiss parents, Jacques Necker, finance minister to King Louis XVI, and his wife, Suzanne Corchod. She conducted a literary salon in Paris, which young Germaine attended and in which she participated. Her parents married her at age twenty to the Swedish ambassador to France, Eric de Staël-Holstein. She had three children, although the youngest was probably the child of her lover Benjamin Constant. Her marriage of convenience lasted until 1797, when the couple separated.

Around the time of her marriage, Germaine had already written two plays. She established her own literary salon, which was known for its liberal political leanings. She favored British-style constitutional monarchy because of her attachment to Montesquieu's political views, which she shared with her father. Although her husband's diplomatic status protected her in the early years of the French Revolution, she did leave the country from 1792 to 1794. When she returned, she reopened her salon and began publishing literary treatises, including *Essay on Fiction* (1795), where she explored the future of the novel. Initially a supporter of the revolution, she grew disenchanted and eventually came to despise Napoleon. Her salon's reputation for its anti-Napoleon sentiment eventually led him to exile her in late 1803. She remained in exile for the next ten years. Initially, she traveled and then settled at the family estate, Coppet, near Lake Geneva, which became a magnet for intellectuals from around Europe, including Byron.

During her trip to Germany 1803–1804, she met the leading German Romantics including the Schlegels. August Wilhelm returned with her to Switzerland, briefly, as the tutor to her children. She had developed an enthusiasm for German culture, because of her lover Benjamin Constant's fascination with it. The trip and his influence eventually led to her most important publication, *Germany* (1810), a serious investigation of German manners, morals, and culture. It is heavily biased in favor of Germany and it is no wonder that Napoleon had those copies found in France burned. She felt the absence of a centralized German government allowed its intellectuals to realize their potential as gifted artists. She is credited with introducing German poetry and philosophy to the non-German-speaking public.

Shortly before her exile, she had published her first autobiographical novel, *Delphine* (1802), which might be termed a sociological study of her world. In 1807, her second novel *Corinne* appeared. It contrasted the world of northern and southern Europe and was written shortly after her visit in Italy. During her exile, she had traveled to Germany, Italy, Austria, Russia, Finland, Sweden, and England. She was disappointed in the Paris she returned to in 1814 after the Bourbon restoration, nevertheless, she remained active as a writer working on her memoirs, *Dix Années in Exil* (*Ten Years in Exile* [1821]) and another study *Considerations of the French Revolution* (1818). She died in Paris in 1817.

Richard Wagner (1813–1883)

The master of German Romantic opera, Wagner was born in Leipzig and grew up in a family of singers and actors. Self-taught at the piano, he enjoyed Mozart's and Beethoven's music. As a Leipzig University music student, rather than attend classes, he spent time alone studying Beethoven. In 1833, he took a job as concert master in Magdeburg and fell in love with actress Wilhelmine (Minna) Planer, whom he eventually married. In the late 1830s, he held several concert master posts, ending up in Riga (Latvia) in 1839.

Constantly in debt, he and Minna left the city by ship ahead of his creditors and settled in Paris. Hoping to make a name there, he spent three penurious years, supporting himself with hack journalism. While in Paris, Wagner was exposed to the rich musical texture of works by Hector Berlioz. During that time he began two operas, *Rienzi* (1840) and *The Flying Dutchman* (1841), the latter the story of a ship's captain condemned to forever sail the seas. The opera's famous storm overture was based on Wagner's experiences aboard ship after he had fled Riga.

Wagner went to Dresden to be court conductor and there produced the two operas begun in Paris. Although the critics did not like them, the audiences did. In 1845, Wagner wrote and produced *Tannhäuser*. His support for the revolutionary events of 1848–1849 led to an arrest warrant being issued for him. He fled to Switzerland and remained an exile until 1860. While in Switzerland, he spent time reading Old Norse sagas and composing related poems, upon which he later based his operas. He wrote music theory as well. *Opera and Drama* (1850–1851) articulated his idea of the *Gesamt-kunstwerk* (the complete work of art), where the music, lyrics, sets, and costumes came together as a unified work through the efforts of a single, creative mind. He also began writing the music for *The Ring of the Nibelung*. Its four operas, *Rhinegold*, *The Valkyrie*, *Sigfried*, and, *The Twilight of the Gods*, reveal Wagner at his most mature. In true Romantic fashion, these operas express personal emotions and national passions.

In 1864, King Ludwig II of Bavaria (ruled 1864–1886) became Wagner's patron. Wagner initially moved to Munich but quickly had to leave because of his flagrant affair with Cosima Liszt von Bülow (1837–1930). Relocated to Lake Lucerne, he completed *The Ring* and oversaw successful productions of his operas in Munich over the next six years. He also sought donations to build a proper house for his operas and, with the king's help, selected a site. Ground breaking occurred in 1872, and, in 1876, the Bayreuth Festival Hall staged the first complete production of *The Ring*. The stories upon which the operas are based are reduced dramatically to a few significant scenes, and the operas' real action comes from the characters' psychological motives. The music's leitmotifs clearly signal the characters' changing feelings. The Romantic theme of redemption through love is one part of *The Ring*, which also addresses timeless political, philosophical, and religious issues.

Wagner married Cosima in 1870, shortly after her divorce. (His wife Minna had died in 1866.) His last opera, *Parsifal*, was produced in 1882. Wagner, by then, had begun having heart trouble. He died a year later while in Venice with his family and was buried at his estate in Bayreuth.

Dorothy Wordsworth (1771–1855)

Born in northwestern England, Dorothy was the middle child of five and the only daughter of John Wordsworth and his wife Anne Cookson. Her father, an attorney, served as a land agent for a local nobleman; unfortunately, her mother's death in 1778 split up the siblings. Her older brothers were sent to school, and she moved in with her mother's cousin, where she spent almost ten years. Her cousin belonged to a Dissenting church and also ran a lending library from her clothing shop. As a result, Dorothy became an enthusiastic reader, used to active household debates.

In 1787, she moved to her maternal grandparents' residence, where she was reacquainted with her brothers and became friends with Mary Hutchinson (who would eventually marry William). In 1794, Dorothy received a small legacy that allowed her to establish a shared household with William in southwestern England. In 1797, William and Dorothy moved near the village where Samuel Taylor Coleridge lived. Here Dorothy wrote her "Alfoxden Journals" (1897), which carefully trace the lives and work of her brother and Coleridge during the first half of 1798, prior to the publication of *Lyrical Ballads* (1798).

The Wordsworth siblings traveled with Coleridge to Germany in September 1798. After returning to England, they finally settled in the Lake District. In May 1800, Dorothy began another journal, the "Grasmere Journals 1800–1803" (1889), in which she recounted the idiosyncrasies of daily life in a small village and the beauty of the natural surroundings. Many of her comments purportedly served as inspiration for her brother's and Coleridge's poetry.

In 1802, William added his bride Mary Hutchinson to the household. The three Wordsworths apparently led a harmonious life, Dorothy acting like a third parent to the children. Dorothy recounted in her journals how she and Mary shared domestic chores and performed secretarial duties for William. Dorothy continued to write as she fulfilled responsibilities to the growing household. In 1803, she, her brother, and Coleridge made a six-week tour of the Scottish Lowlands and the southwestern Highlands. Her journal *Reflections on a Tour in Scotland* (1879) reveals her acute powers of observation as she describes the unspoiled landscapes. Another journal she kept in 1805 describes a walking tour of the Lake District, which she took with William. He used some of her observations in his *Guide to the Lakes* (1810), which enjoyed great popularity.

In 1829, a serious illness left Dorothy in frail health, and by 1835, she began to suffer from dementia. Since she had an established position within William's household, Dorothy remained there. The last twenty years of her life, she spent in an increasing mental haze. She died in 1855.

William Wordsworth (1770–1850)

William Wordsworth was the second of five children born to attorney and land agent John Wordsworth and his wife Anne Cookson. Wordsworth's mother died when he was eight, and he and his siblings were sent off to school or to live with relatives. William attended a grammar school in Hawkshead, in England's Lake District, where he wandered the countryside and learned to love nature. In 1781, his guardians encouraged Wordsworth to begin either legal or theological studies at Cambridge, where he was an indifferent student. During the summer of 1790, he made his first trip to the Continent. The trip began in France, then involved in the early stages of its revolution. To Wordsworth, the ideas associated with the French Revolution represented the dawn of a new era. Later, in Switzerland, he crossed the Simplon Pass, an important experience of the sublime, which he later recounted. He graduated from Cambridge in January 1791 and returned to France. Growing estranged from the revolution's increasing radicalism, Wordsworth returned to England in December 1792. Between 1792 and 1795, he struggled to find his niche; eventually, he and his sister Dorothy established a household in southwestern England, and at this time, he recognized his vocation as a writer.

Wordsworth apparently met Samuel Taylor Coleridge in 1795. The two could not have been more different. Coleridge, animated, often unstable, but at the same time brilliant, contrasted sharply with the introspective and deliberate Wordsworth. By 1797, Wordsworth and Dorothy had established residence in Alfoxden House near Coleridge. This proximity led to close collaboration between the two, resulting in the *Lyrical Ballads*, which appeared anonymously in 1798 and changed poetic standards of the day. Initially, the book did not receive much attention.

During the winter of 1798–1799, Wordsworth, his sister, and Coleridge traveled to Germany, where he began work on *The Prelude*. By the end of 1799, living in Grasmere in the Lake District,

Wordsworth wrote, revised poetry, and continued with his master-piece, *The Prelude*. Part of this effort involved writing a "Preface" to *Lyrical Ballads*, which explained the "experimental" nature of the poetry. In 1802, an inheritance finally gave him the security that allowed him to marry Mary Hutchinson.

In 1805, Wordsworth completed *The Prelude* and a poetry volume. While the former remained unpublished during his lifetime, the latter, *Poems in Two Volumes* (1806), firmly established his reputation as a poet. It contained "Ode: Intimations of Immortality," which commemorates the death of Wordsworth's brother John, a sea captain who had drowned in a shipwreck. Deeply affected by his brother's death, Wordsworth's subsequent poetry took on a more somber tone, and some critics feel the quality declined. In 1813, he accepted a minor government job which gave him much needed income but did not force him to give up writing poetry. During his later years, Wordsworth received numerous visitors at his residence, who wanted to be inspired by the great man. In 1843, he became Poet Laureate of Britain, a position which his acquaintance Robert Southey (1784–1843) had held for the previous thirty years. Wordsworth died in 1850 from the effects of a cold.

PRIMARY DOCUMENTS

Document 1: Jean-Jacques Rousseau, from
The Confessions: Book Three (1731–1732)

Jean-Jacques Rousseau (1712–1778), orphaned early in life, came to his career as a political and social critic and author by a circuitous route. After leaving his native Geneva as a teenager, he eventually came to reside with Madame Louise de Warens (1699–1768) at her estate Chambéry. He was nineteen and she was thirty-two at the time, and he resided there off and on for over a decade. She helped him develop the social graces that later allowed him to mix in good company, and the two also became lovers. In 1742, he established himself in Paris, a struggling author seeking fame and fortune. He associated with the *philosophes* and gained prominence when he won a prize for his essay *A Discourse on the Sciences and the Arts* in 1750. He went on to write several novels and his political treatise *The Social Contract*, which were published in the 1760s. His *Confessions* (1781–1788) became a best seller, in part because he was so frank in his discussions about his private life, which included numerous affairs and genuinely disgusting behavior. In the selection that follows, he describes his beloved "Mamma," Madame de Warens and life at her home. He explains his love for her and how he sought solace from nature, when he could not be with her.

> The arrangement of her housekeeping was exactly what I would have chosen, and I shared it with satisfaction. I was least pleased with the necessity of remaining too long at table. Madame de Warrens was so much incommoded with the first smell of the soup or meat, as almost to occasion fainting; from this she slowly recovered, talking meantime, and never attempting to eat for the first half hour. I could have dined thrice in the time, and had ever finished a meal long before she began; I then ate again for company; and though by this means I usually dined twice,

felt no inconvenience from it. In short, I was perfectly at my ease, and the happier as my situation required no care. Not being at this time instructed in the state of her finances, I supposed her means were adequate to her expense; and though I afterwards found the same abundance, yet when instructed in her real situation, finding her pension ever anticipated, prevented me from enjoying the same tranquillity. Foresight with me has always embittered enjoyment; in vain I saw the approach of misfortunes, I was never the more likely to avoid them.

From the first moment of our meeting, the softest familiarity was established between us, and in the same degree it continued during the rest of her life. Child was my name, Mamma was hers, and child and mamma we have ever continued, even after a number of years had almost effaced the apparent difference of age between us. I think those names convey an exact idea of our behavior, the simplicity of our manners, and, above all, the similarity of our dispositions. To me she was the tenderest of mothers, ever preferring my welfare to her own pleasure; and if my own satisfaction found some interest in my attachment to her, it was not to change its nature, but only to render it more exquisite, and infatuate me with the charm of having a mother young and handsome, whom I was delighted to caress: I say literally, to caress, for never did it enter into her imagination to deny me the tenderest maternal kisses and endearments, or into my heart to abuse them. It will be said, our connection was of a different kind: I confess it;....[1]

The sudden sight of her, on our first interview, was the only truly passionate moment she ever inspired me with; and even that was principally the work of surprise. My indiscreet glances never went searching beneath her neckerchief, although the ill-concealed plumpness was quite attractive for them. With her I had neither transports nor desires, but remained in a ravishing calm, sensible of a happiness I could not define.

She was the only person with whom I never experienced that want of conversation, which to me is so painful to endure. Our *tête-à-têtes* were rather an inexhaustible chat than conversation, which could only conclude from interruption. So far from finding discourse difficult, I rather thought it a hardship to be silent unless, when contemplating her projects, she sank into a reverie; while I silently let her meditate, and gazing on her, was the happiest of men. I had another singular fancy, which was that without pretending to the favor of a *tête-à-tête*, I was perpetually seeking occasion to form them, enjoying such opportunities with rapture; and when importunate visitors broke in upon us, no matter whether it was a man or woman, I went out murmuring, not being able to remain a secondary object in her company; then, counting the minutes in her antechamber, I used to curse these eternal visitors, thinking it inconceivable how they could find so much to say, for I had still more.

If ever I felt the full force of my attachment, it was when I did not see her. When in her presence, I was only content; when absent, my uneasiness reaching almost to melancholy, and a wish to live with her gave me emotions of tenderness even to tears. Never shall I forget one great holiday, while she was at vespers, when I took a walk out of the city, my heart full of her image, and an ardent wish to pass my life with her. I could easily enough see that at present this was impossible; that the happiness I enjoyed would be of short duration, and this idea gave to my contemplations a tincture of melancholy, which however, was not gloomy, but tempered with a flattering hope. The ringing of bells, which ever particularly affects me, the singing of birds, the fineness of the day, the beauty of the landscape, the scattered country houses, among which in idea I placed our future dwelling, altogether struck me with an impression so lively, tender, melancholy, and powerful, that I saw myself in ecstasy transported into that happy time and abode, where my heart, possessing all the felicity it could desire, might taste it with raptures inexpressible. I never recollect to have enjoyed the future with such a force of illusion as at that time; and what has particularly struck me in the recollection of this reverie is that, when realized, I found my situation exactly as I had imagined it. If ever waking dream had an appearance of a prophetic vision, it was assuredly this; I was only deceived in its imaginary duration, for days, years, and life itself, passed ideally in perfect tranquillity, while the reality lasted but a moment. Alas! My most durable happiness was but as a dream, which I had no sooner had a glimpse of, than I instantly awoke.

I know not when I should have done, if I was to enter into a detail of all the follies that affection for my dear Madam de Warrens made me commit. When absent from her, how often have I kissed the bed on a supposition that she had slept there; the curtains and all the furniture of my chamber, on recollecting they were hers, and that her charming hands had touched them; nay, the floor itself, when I considered she had walked there.[2] Sometimes even in her presence extravagancies escaped me, which only the most violent passions seemed capable of inspiring; in a word, there was but one essential difference to distinguish me from an absolute lover, and that particularly renders my situation almost inconceivable.

Source: Jean-Jacques Rousseau, *The Confessions of Jean-Jacques Rousseau,* trans. W. Conyngham Mallory (New York: Tudor Publishing, 1928), 155–159.

Document 2: Edmund Burke, from *On the Sublime and the Beautiful* (1757)

Edmund Burke (1729–1797), political writer and statesman, grew up in Ireland, the son of a Protestant father and a Catholic mother. He attended Trinity College in Dublin for two years before moving to London in 1750 to begin legal studies. He apparently lost interest in those studies and traveled around England and France. In 1757, his *A Philosophical Enquiry into the Origin of Our Ideas of the Sublime and the Beautiful* appeared and British and Continental intellectuals recognized its contribution to aesthetics. He founded *The Annual Register*, which discussed world affairs, in 1758. At this time Burke associated with some of England's leading literary figures, including Oliver Goldsmith (1730?–1774) and Dr. Samuel Johnson (1709–1784).

He began his political career in 1765 as a member of the House of Commons, associated with the Whigs. Burke believed that King George III (ruled 1760–1820) was asserting too much executive authority. In *Thoughts on the Cause of the Present Discontents* (1770), Burke commented on the royal prerogative and also justified the existence of political parties, which he regarded as a critical link between king and Parliament. He continued to serve in Parliament and in the mid-1770s spoke out against the crown's treatment of the North American colonies. His interest in governance over colonies led him to try to alleviate economic burdens placed on his native Ireland and also to ensure that the British East India Company carried out its duties in India according to its charter. He eventually aligned himself with a proposal to create a board of independent commissioners, who would rule India from London.

When the French Revolution broke out in 1789, Burke initially reserved judgment, but then he came to despise it and the favorable reaction it had received from many in England. He wrote *Reflections on the Revolution in France* (1790) in which he ridiculed the revolution's leaders for destroying established institutions and predicted that their actions would lead to regicide and dictatorship. He lived to see his predictions come true.

In his essay on aesthetics, *A Philosophical Enquiry into the Origin of Our Ideas of the Sublime and the Beautiful*, he explores how the senses, the imagination, and judgment interrelate in order to appreciate art. To understand the sublime and beautiful, one must examine the experience of pain and pleasure. Pain is more powerful than pleasure and has greater influence on an individual's imagination. He goes on to define the sublime and the beautiful and then to explore how they combine to make works of art inspiring. This selection highlights some aspects of his definition of sublime.

Part II. Section VII.—"Vastness"

Greatness of dimension is a powerful cause of the sublime. This is too evident, and the observation too common, to need any illustration: it is not so common to consider in what ways greatness of dimension, vastness of extent or quantity, has the most striking effect. For certainly, there are ways and modes, wherein the same quantity of extension shall produce greater effects than it is found to do in others. Extension is either in length, height, or depth. Of these the length strikes least; an hundred yards of even ground will never work such an effect as a tower an hundred yards high, or a rock or mountain of that altitude. I am apt to imagine likewise, that height is less grand than depth; and that we are more struck at looking down from a precipice, than looking up at an object of equal height; but of that I am not very positive. A perpendicular has more force in forming the sublime, than an inclined plane; and the effects of a rugged and broken surface seem stronger than where it is smooth and polished. . . .

Part II. Section XIII.—"Magnificence"

Magnificence is likewise a source of the sublime. A great profusion of things, which are splendid or valuable in themselves, is *magnificent*. The starry heaven, though it occurs so very frequently to our view, never fails to excite an idea of grandeur. This cannot be owing to the stars themselves, separately considered. The number is certainly the cause. The apparent disorder augments the grandeur, for the appearance of care is highly contrary to our idea of magnificence. Besides, the stars lie in such apparent confusion, as makes it impossible on ordinary occasions to reckon them. This gives them the advantage of a sort of infinity. In works or art, this kind of grandeur, which consists in multitude, is to be very courteously admitted; because a profusion of excellent things is not to be attained, or with too much difficulty; and because in many cases this splendid confusion would destroy all use, which should be attended to in most of the works of art with the greatest care; besides, it is to be considered, that unless you can produce an appearance of infinity by your disorder, you will have disorder only without magnificence. There are, however, a sort of fireworks, and some other things, that in this way succeed well, and are truly grand. There are also many descriptions in the poets and orators, which owe their sublimity to a richness and profusion of images, in which the mind is so dazzled as to make it impossible to attend to the exact coherence and agreement of the allusions, which we should require on every other occasion.…

Source: Edmund Burke, *On Taste; On the Sublime and the Beautiful; Reflections on the French Revolution; and A Letter to a Noble Lord; with Introduction, Notes, and Illustrations,* Harvard Classics, vol. 24 (New York: P. F. Collier and Son, 1909), 61, 66.

Document 3: Johann Wolfgang von Goethe, from *The Sorrows of Young Werther* (1774)

Germany's greatest author, Johann Wolfgang von Goethe (1749–1832), like Beethoven, defies rigid classification in terms of his aesthetic style. Personally, he regarded himself as a Classical author, but his long career and varied literary works have been associated with the *Sturm und Drang*, the Classical Era, and the Age of Romanticism. Although Goethe practiced law at the completion of his university studies, his real devotion was to literature. His drama *Götz von Berlichingen* (1773) is regarded as the first "work of genius" of the *Sturm und Drang*. Dealing with depression because of his unrequited love for Charlotte Buff, Goethe wrote the epistolary novel *The Sorrows of Young Werther* (1774), an inspiration for many Romantics. It proved cathartic for him, but started a cult of morbidity and a series of suicides among impressionable young men, who felt they suffered as had Werther. The selection that follows reveals Werther's torment as explained in his last letter to his beloved Charlotte, which he writes shortly before he kills himself, and the aftermath of his suicide.

See Charlotte, I do not shudder to take the cold and fatal cup, from which I shall drink the draught of death. Your hand presents it to me, and I do not tremble. All, all is now concluded: the wishes and the hopes of my existence are fulfilled. With cold, unflinching hand I knock at the brazen portals of Death.

Oh, that I had enjoyed the bliss of dying for you! How gladly would I have sacrificed myself for you, Charlotte! And could I but restore peace and joy to your bosom, with what resolution, with what joy, would I not meet my fate! But it is the lot of only a chosen few to shed their blood for their friends, and by their death to augment, a thousand times, the happiness of those by whom they are beloved.

I wish, Charlotte, to be buried in the dress I wear at present: it has been rendered sacred by your touch. I have begged this favor of your father. My spirit soars above my sepulcher. I do not wish my pockets to be searched. The knot of pink ribbon which you wore on your bosom the first time I saw you, surrounded by the children—Oh, kiss them a thousand times for me, and tell them the fate of their unhappy friend! I think I see them playing around me. The dear Children! How warmly have I been attached to you, Charlotte! Since the first hour I saw you, how impossible have I found it to leave you. This ribbon must be buried with me: it was a present from you on my birthday. How confused it all appears! Little did I then think that I should journey this road. But peace! I pray you, peace!

They are loaded—the clock strikes twelve. I say amen. Charlotte, Charlotte! Farewell, farewell!

A neighbor saw the flash, and heard the report of the pistol; but as every thing remained quiet, he thought no more of it.

In the morning, at six o'clock, the servant went into Werther's room with a candle. He found his master stretched upon the floor, weltering in his blood, and the pistols at his side. He called, he took him in his arms, but received no answer. Life was not yet quite extinct. The servant ran for a surgeon, and then went to fetch Albert. Charlotte heard the ringing of the bell: a cold shudder seized her. She wakened her husband, and they both rose. The servant, bathed in tears, faltered forth the dreadful news. Charlotte fell senseless at Albert's feet.

When the surgeon came to the unfortunate Werther, he was still lying on the floor; and his pulse beat, but his limbs were cold. The bullet, entering the forehead over the right eye, had penetrated the skull. A vein was opened in his right arm: the blood came, and he still continued to breathe.

From the blood which flowed from the chair, it could be inferred that he had committed the rash act sitting at his bureau, and that he afterwards fell upon the floor. He was found lying on his back near the window. He was in full-dress costume.

The house, the neighborhood, and the whole town were immediately in commotion. Albert arrived. They had laid Werther on the bed: his head was bound up, and the paleness of death was upon his face. His limbs were motionless; but he still breathed, at one time strongly, then weaker—his death was momently expected.

He had drunk only one glass of the wine. "Emilia Galotti" [a drama by Gotthold Ephraim Lessing (1729–1781)] lay open upon his bureau.

I shall say nothing of Albert's distress, or of Charlotte's grief.

The old steward hastened to the house immediately upon hearing the news; he embraced his dying friend among a flood of tears. His eldest boys soon followed him on foot. In speech-less sorrow they threw themselves on their knees by the bedside, and kissed his hands and face. The eldest, who was his favorite, hung over him till he expired; and even then he was removed by force. At twelve o'clock Werther breathed his last. The presence of the steward, and the precautions he had adopted, prevented a disturbance; and that night, at the hour of eleven, he caused the body to be interred in the place which Werther had selected for himself.

The steward and his sons followed the corpse to the grave. Albert was unable to accompany them. Charlotte's life was despaired of. The body was carried by laborers. No priest attended.

Source: Johann Wolfgang von Goethe, *The Sorrows of Young Werther; Elective Affinities; and A Novelette*, Household Edition (New York: John D. Williams, 1882), 108–109.

Document 4: Johann Gottlieb Fichte, from *Addresses to the German Nation* (1808)

Johann Gottlieb Fichte (1762–1814) greatly admired Immanuel Kant's philosophical views including the idea of man's inherent moral worth. Caught up like many intellectuals in the possibilities associated with reform as a result of the French Revolution, Fichte wrote a political work entitled *Contribution to the Correction of the Public's Judgments Regarding the French Revolution* (1793), where he discussed how political liberty was fitting for the "intelligent agent" man. In that year, he took a teaching position at the University of Jena, where he remained for five years. His association with a journal which published an article purported to endorse atheism led to his expulsion. He then moved to the University of Berlin, where he taught from 1799 to 1806. During his years at Jena, his philosophical focus was ethics, while in Berlin, he turned to a more mystical perspective and came to believe that religious faith was more important than moral reason. The Napoleonic victory over Prussia in 1806 drove Fichte from Berlin and he eventually relocated to Copenhagen. When he returned to Berlin in August 1807, he turned to more practical matters in his scholarly work. He got involved with a plan to create a new university in Berlin and about that time he began delivering a series of lectures, which were collected as *Reden an die deutsche Nation* (1808) (*Addresses to the German Nation* [English translation 1922]), which outlined his ideas about how to cultivate German national pride. Interestingly enough, the work passed French censors, because they saw it as a treatise on education. Fichte's ideas resurfaced among the nationalist arguments espoused by the leaders of the Revolution of 1848 and subsequent events such as the unification of Germany in 1870–1871 and the rise of Nazism. In the hands of the Nazis, Fichte's ideas were mutated into justifying German aggression in the name of German *Volk* (people). The following includes segments from the Twelfth Lecture entitled: "The Means to sustain Ourselves until We Achieve our Main Goal," which discusses national identity and education among other topics.

> We must overcome the sweetness of servitude because it robs the next generation of the hope of liberation.... We have to lift our thoughts to freedom....
>
> Ask me how we should accomplish this, the all-encompassing answer is this: we must become what we should become: Germans! We should not subdue our spirit, we must develop in ourselves a strong and certain spirit; we must be serious in all matters and must not proceed in a thoughtless way and become a laughing stock. We must build lasting and unshakable principles that support our thoughts and actions. Life and thought with us should be indivisible and a penetrating and solid whole. We must be measured in our nature and our truth and throw out artificial foreign things. We must, to say it simply, have to develop our character; to be German is without doubt the same thing....
>
> These speeches have invited you and invited all Germans, insofar at that is possible through their publication, to gather themselves together, in order to make a hard and fast decision and to unite themselves over the following questions: 1. Whether it is true or not that a German nation exists and that its continued existence as an independent and special entity is in danger. 2. Whether it is worth the trouble or not to preserve the German nation? 3. Whether a certain and far-reaching means exists to aid this preservation and what is this means?

Source: Johann Gottlieb Fichte, *Fichte Reden an die Deutsche Nation* (Berlin: Deutsche Bibliothek, 1912), 208–209, 210 (translated by Joanne Schneider).

Document 5: William Blake, "The Chimney Sweeper" (1794)

William Blake (1757–1827), in part because of his religious background, was very sensitive to the human condition. He had been raised a Dissenter, one of those individuals who disagreed with the established Church of England. He believed neither the Church nor the British government were doing anything on behalf of society's poor. In 1789 and 1794, his volumes of lyrical poetry, *Songs of Innocence* and his *Songs of Experience*, appeared and recounted Blake's world view. The former highlighted the joys of childhood, while the latter investigated more serious issues. Some poems directly addressed social concerns of the day, including widespread poverty. He believed that part of the poet's duty was to make people aware of problems such as the plight of poor children. "The Chimney Sweeper" appeared in *Songs of Experience*. While many anthologies present a shorter version of the poem, the expanded one from the Ellis collection highlights the dilemma of these impoverished, forgotten boys.

When my mother died when I was very young
And my father sold me while yet my tongue
Could scarcely cry "'weep! 'weep! 'weep 'weep!!"
So your chimneys I sweep & in soot I sleep.

There's little Tom Dacre, who cried when his head,
That curl'd like a lamb's back, was shav'd: so I said
"Hush, Tom! Never mind it, for when your head's bare
You know that the soot cannot spoil your white hair."

And so he was quiet and that very night,
As Tom was a-sleeping, he had such a sight!
That thousands of sweepers, Dick, Joe, Ned and Jack,
Were all of them lock'd up in coffins of black.

And by came an Angel who had a bright key,
And he open'd the coffins and set them all free;
Then down a green plain leaping, laughing, they run,
And wash in a river, and shine in the sun.

Then naked and white, all their bags left behind,
They rise upon clouds and sport in the wind:
And the angel told Tom, if he'd be a good boy,
He's have God for his father and never want joy.

And so Tom awoke, and we rose in the dark,
And got with our bags and brushes to work.
Though the morning was cold, Tom was happy and warm:
So if all do their duty they need not fear harm.

Source: William Blake, *The Poetical Works of William Blake*, vol. 1, ed. Edwin J. Ellis (London: Chatto and Windus, 1906), 67–68.

Document 6: William Wordsworth, "We Are Seven" (1798)

William Wordsworth's (1770–1850) uncles believed that he should embark on a career as an Anglican priest, so as a child and youth he attended very good schools, where he received a Classical education, including exposure to the types of poetry popular in eighteenth century Britain. Wordsworth found the language of such poetry artificial as well as elitist, because of its Classical allusions. When he began to write poetry, he rebelled against this formalism. In the "Preface" to *Lyrical Ballads* (1800), he stated that he felt that poetry should be written in an accessible language. So, many of his more touching poems are written in simple English and often tell stories of ordinary people. Such is the case with "We Are Seven," written in Alfoxden in the Spring of 1798 and based upon an encounter Wordsworth had had with a little girl five years earlier. This poem appeared in the first edition of *Lyrical Ballads* (1798).

—A simple Child,
That lightly draws its breath,
And feels its life in every limb,
What should it know of death?

I met a little cottage Girl:
She was eight years old, she said;
Her hair was thick with many a curl
That clustered round her head.

She had a rustic, woodland air,
And she was wildly clad:
Her eyes were fair, and very fair;
—Her beauty made me glad.

"Sisters and brothers, little Maid,
How many may you be?"
"How many? Seven in all," she said
And wondering looked at me.

"And where are they? I pray you tell."
She answered, "Seven are we;
And two of us at Conway dwell,
And two are gone to sea.

"Two of us in the church-yard lie,
My sister and my brother;
And, in the church-yard cottage, I
Dwell near them with my mother."

"You say that two at Conway dwell,
And two are gone to sea,
Yet ye are seven!—I pray you tell,
Sweet Maid, how this may be."

Then did the little Maid reply,
"Seven boys and girls are we;
Two of us in the church-yard lie,
Beneath the church-yard tree."

"You run about, my little Maid,
Your limbs they are alive;
If two are in the church-yard laid,
Then ye are only five."

"Their graves are green, they may be seen,"
The little Maid replied,
"Twelve steps or more from my mother's door,
And they are side by side."

"My stockings there I often knit,
My kerchief there I hem;
And there upon the ground I sit,
And sing a song to them.

"And often after sunset, Sir,
When it is light and fair,
I take my little porringer,
And eat my supper there.

"The first that died was sister Jane;
In bed she moaning lay,
Till God released her of her pain;
And then she went away.

"So in the church-yard she was laid;
And, when the grass was dry,
Together round her grave we played,
My brother John and I.

"And when the ground was white with snow,
And I could run and slide,
My brother John was forced to go,
And he lies by her side."

"How many are you, then," said I,
"If they two are in heaven?"
Quick was the little Maid's reply,
"O Master! We are seven."

"But they are dead; those two are dead!
Their spirits are in heaven!"
'Twas throwing words away; for still

The little Maid would have her will,
And said, "Nay, we are seven!"

Source: William Wordsworth, *The Complete Poetical Works of William Wordsworth*, ed. Andrew J. George, Cambridge Edition of the Poets (New York: Houghton, Mifflin and Co., 1904), 73.

Document 7: John Keats, letters to his brother Tom (1818)

Like many Romantic poets, John Keats (1795–1821) sought inspiration from nature and to that end engaged in walking tours of picturesque areas. The following letters come from a trip that he undertook during the summer of 1818 to the Lake District of England and to Scotland. He recounts to his brother various sights and comments on their beauty. He is so taken by the landscape that he does not seem to mind that on one part of the excursion, he got wet because he had slipped in a marshy area. Once in Scotland, he observes a country dance, in which the Scottish customs appear much more boisterous than English counterparts.

Keswick
June 29

My Dear Tom,
    I cannot make my journal as distinct and actual as I could wish, from having been engaged in writing to George [the other brother], and therefore I must tell you, without circumstance that we proceeded from Ambleside to Rydal, saw the waterfalls there, and called on Wordsworth, who was not at home, nor was any one of his family.... The approach to Derwent Water surpassed Windermere: it is richly wooded, and shut in with rich-toned mountains. From Helvellyn to Keswick was eight miles to breakfast, after which we took a complete circuit of the lake, going about ten miles, and seeing on our way the fall of Lodore. I had an easy climb among the streams, about the fragments of rocks, and should have got, I think, to the summit, but unfortunately I was damped by slipping one leg into a squashy hole. There is no great body of water, but the accompaniment is delightful; for it oozes out from a cleft in perpendicular rocks, all fledged with ash and other beautiful trees. It is a strange thing how they got there.... We went to bed rather fatigued, but not so much so as to hinder us getting up this morning to mount Skiddaw. It promised all along to be fair, and we had fagged and tugged nearly to the top, when, at half-past six, there came a mist upon us, and shut out the view. We did not, however, lose anything by it: we were high enough without mist to

see the coast of Scotland, the Irish Sea, the hills beyond Lancaster, and nearly all the large ones of Cumberland and Westmoreland, particularly Helvellyn and Scawfell. It grew colder and colder as we ascended, and we were glad, at about three parts of the way, to taste a little rum which the guide brought with him, mixed mind ye, with mountain water. I took two glasses going and one returning. It is about six miles from where I am writing to the top; so we have walked ten miles before breakfast to-day.

July 1

We are this morning at Carlisle. After Skiddaw, we walked to Treby, the oldest market town in Cumberland, where we were greatly amused by a country dancing-school, holden at the "Tun." It was indeed "no new cotillion fresh from France." No, they kickit and jumpit with mettle extraordinary, and whiskit, and fristkit, and toed it, and go'd it, and twirl'd it, and whirl'd it, and stamped it, and sweated it, tattooing the floor like mad. The difference between our country dances and these Scottish figures is about the same as leisurely stirring a cup of tea and beating up a batter-pudding. I was extremely gratified to think that, if I had pleasures they knew nothing of, they had also some into which I could not possibly enter. I hope I shall not return without having got the Highland fling. There was as fine a row of boys and girls as you ever saw; some beautiful faces, and one exquisite mouth. I never felt so near the glory of patriotism, the glory of making, by any mean, a country happier. This is what I like better than scenery. I fear our continued moving from place to place will prevent our becoming learned in village affairs: we are mere creatures of rivers, lakes, and mountains. Our yesterday's journey was from Treby to Wigton, and from Wigton to Carlisle. The cathedral does not appear very fine; the castle is very ancient, and of brick. The city is very various: old, white-washed narrow streets, broad, red-brick ones, more modern. I will tell you anon whether the inside of the cathedral is worth looking at. It is built of sandy red stone, or brick. We have now walked 114 miles, and are merely a little tired in the thighs and a little blistered. We shall ride 38 miles to Dumfries, when we shall linger while about Nithsdale and Galoway....

Source: Lord Houghton, ed., *The Life and Letters of John Keats: A New Edition* (London: Edward Moxon and Co., 1867), 132–134.

Document 8: Felicia Hemans, "The Last Song of Sappho" (ca. 1830)

When she was fourteen Felicia Browne Hemans (1793–1835) published a collection, *Poems* (1808), which was criticized as an adolescent girl's effort. Four years later, shortly before her marriage, she published *The Domestic Affections and Other Poems*. Despite five pregnancies in six years, Hemans kept writing, inspired by Byron's style. After her husband left her in 1818, she supported herself and children through her poetry and became the best selling English-language poet of the early nineteenth century. In the summer of 1830, she briefly moved to the Lake District, intent on seeking inspiration from William Wordsworth. He apparently had mixed feelings about her, liking some of her poetry, but also faulting her for neglecting her female duties in order to write poetry. In some respects, her ambivalence about being a woman writing poetry comes through "The Last Song of Sappho." Here, Sappho (the Ancient Greek lyric poet), stands by the sea holding the laurel wreath, a prize she has won for her poetry. Despite her fame, she is lonely and sad; even the sea birds have love and a home to return to, while she has nothing. She has poured her heart into writing poetry, but the world has held her at a distance. She hopes the sea will give her peace.

[Suggested by a beautiful sketch, the design of the younger Westmacott. It represents Sappho sitting on a rock above the sea, with her lyre cast at her feet. There is a desolate grace about the whole figure, which seems penetrated with the feeling of utter abandonment.]

SOUND on, thou dark unslumbering sea!
My dirge is in thy moan;
My spirit finds response in thee,
To its own ceaseless cry—'Alone, alone!'
Yet send me back one other word,
Ye tones that never cease!
Oh! let your secret caves be stirr'd,
And say, dark waters! will ye give me *peace?*
Away! my weary soul hath sought
In vain one echoing sigh,
One answer to consuming thought
In human hearts—and will the *wave* reply ?
Sound on, thou dark, unslumbering sea!
Sound in thy scorn and pride!
I ask not, alien world, from thee,
What my own kindred earth hath still denied.
And yet I loved that earth so well,
With all its lovely things!
—Was it for this the death-wind fell
On my rich lyre, and quench'd its living strings?
—Let them lie silent at my feet!
Since broken even as they,
The heart whose music made them sweet,

Hath pour'd on desert-sands its wealth away.
Yet glory's light hath touch'd my name,
The laurel-wreath is mine—
—With a lone heart, a weary frame—
O restless deep! I come to make them thine!
Give to that crown, that burning crown,
Place in thy darkest hold!
Bury my anguish, my renown,
With hidden wrecks, lost gems, and wasted gold.
Thou sea-bird on the billow's crest,
Thou hast thy love, thy home;
They wait thee in the quiet nest,
And I, the unsought, unwatch'd-for—I too come!
I, with this winged nature fraught,
These visions wildly free,
This boundless love, this fiery thought—
Alone I come—oh! give me peace, dark sea!

Source: Felicia Hemans, *The Poetical Works of Felicia Hemans, Complete in One Volume* (Philadelphia: Porter and Coates, 1853), 609.

Document 9: E. T. A. Hoffmann, from "Master Martin, the Cooper, and His Journeyman" (1818)

E. T. A. Hoffmann (1776–1822) had many careers, before finally deciding to devote himself to writing short fiction. He trained as a lawyer and served in various government posts, at the same time, he was composing music, writing music criticism, conducting music, and writing prose. He is most well-known for short stories or his tales. Hoffmann used the folk tale model for his stories and like many Romantics set them in the Middle Ages. In some, he examines the artist and his relationship to the world. Is the artist of this world or beyond it? His macabre stories have remained quite popular, but he also wrote more straightforward tales, including "Master Martin, the Cooper, and his Journeyman," which appeared in a collection entitled *Die Serapionsbrüder* (*The Serapion Brethren*, 4 vols. 1819–1821). It is set in medieval Nuremberg and tells the story of a cooper, Master Martin, his beautiful daughter Rose, and the young journeyman Frederick, who has fallen in love with her. The world of the medieval *Minnesänger* (minstrels) also highlights this story, which later became an inspiration for Richard Wagner's opera *Die Meistersinger von Nürnberg* The following selection begins the conclusion of the story: Frederick has given up hope of marrying Rose, because his first love is being a goldsmith, rather than being a cooper. Martin had claimed that a deathbed statement from Rose's grandmother had told him that she would marry a cooper—or so he thought. The clue rests in the words of the poem that the dying woman had quoted to Martin.

> However angry Master Martin might feel towards Reinhold (a friend of Frederick's and fellow apprentice) and Frederick, he could not but admit that along with them all joy and all pleasure had disappeared from the workshop. Every day he was annoyed and provoked by the new journeymen. He had to look after every little trifle, and it cost him no end of trouble and exertion to get even the smallest amount of work done to his mind [the way he wanted]. Quite tired out with the cares of the day, he often sighted, "O Reinhold! O Frederick!" I wish you had not so shamefully deceived me, I wish you had been good coopers." Things got so bad that he often contemplated the idea of giving up business altogether. [Martin is then visited by a city official Herr Paumgartner and Master Holzschuer, the goldsmith, with whom Frederick is now working. They encourage him to allow Frederick to marry Rose, but Martin refuses. Holzschuer announces Frederick's intention to leave town and his wish to give Rose a gift.] Whereupon Master Holzschuer produced a small artistically-chased silver cup, and handed it to Master Martin, who, a great lover of costly vessels and such like, took it and examined it on all sides with much satisfaction. And indeed a more splendid piece of silver work than this little cup could hardly be seen. Delicate chains of vine-leaves and roses were intertwined round about it, and pretty angels peeped up out of the roses and the bursting buds, whilst within, on the gilded bottom of the cup, were engraved angels lovingly caressing each other. And when the clear bright wine was poured into the cup, the little angels seemed to dance up and down as if playing prettily together. "It is indeed an elegant piece of work," said Master Martin, "and I will keep it if Frederick will take the double of what it is worth in good gold pieces." Thus speaking, he filled the cup and raised it to his lips. At this moment the door was softly opened, and Frederick stepping in, his countenance pale and stamped with the bitter, bitter pain of separating for ever from her he held dearest on earth. As soon as Rose saw him she uttered a loud piercing cry, "O my dearest Frederick!" and fell almost fainting on his breast. Master Martin set down the cup, and on seeing Rose in Frederick's arms opened his eyes wide as if he saw a ghost. Then he again took up the cup without speaking a word, and looked into it; but all at once he leapt from his seat and cried in a loud voice, "Rose, Rose, do you love Frederick?" "Oh!" whispered Rose, "I cannot any longer conceal it, I love him as I love my own life; my heart nearly broke when you sent him away." "Then embrace your betrothed, Frederick; yes, yes, your betrothed Frederick," cried Master Martin. Paumgartner

and Holzschuser looked at each other utterly bewildered with astonishment, but Master Martin, holding the cup in his hand, went on, "by the good God, has it not all come to pass as the old lady prophesied?—

'A vessel fair to see he'll bring,
In which the spicy liquid foams,
And bright, bright angels gaily sing,
... The vessel fair with golden grace
Lo! Him who brings it in the house,
Thou wilt reward with sweet embrace,
And, an thy lover be but true,
Thou need'st not wait thy father's kiss.'

O stupid fool I have been! Here is the vessel fair to see, the angels—the lover—ay! Ay! Gentlemen; it's all right now, all right now; my son-in-law is found."

Source: *Weird Tales by E. T. A. Hoffmann: A New Translation from the German with a Biographical Memoir*, vol. 2, trans. J. T. Bealby (New York: Charles Scribner's Sons, 1890), 141–144.

Document 10: Ann Radcliffe, from *The Mysteries of Udolfo* (1794)

Ann Ward Radcliffe (1764–1823) was born into a shopkeeper's family in London. When she was about eight the family moved to Bath, where as an only child, she spent much time alone. Largely self-educated, Ann wrote to amuse herself. In 1787, she married William Radcliffe, who became the publisher of the *English Chronicle*. Because her husband devoted long hours to his journal, Ann had considerable free time. An avid reader, she decided to write novels. Whereas her first, *The Castles of Athlen and Dunbayne*, took place in Scotland, the other eight were set against the eerie, mountainous backgrounds of the Pyrenees, the Alps, and the Apennines in Europe. Interestingly enough, she only traveled abroad once and visited Holland and the Rhineland areas of Germany.

Her fourth novel, *The Mysteries of Udolfo* (1794), is dominated by the Romantic theme of the sublime. Emily falls in love with the young nobleman Valancourt when he accompanies her and her father as they travel through forest and mountain landscapes. For female writers, experiencing the sublime by viewing the grandeur and power of nature was not a frightening event but an empowering one. It inspired and cultivated love, because each person experiencing the sublime acquired a sense of personal worth.[3]

The following selections describe Emily and Valancourt reminiscing about their trip through the mountains when they first met and experienced the sublime and his subsequent declaration of love, and then Emily experiencing a mysterious scene at Castle Udolpho at night.

Emily and Valancourt talked of the scenes they had passed among the Pyrenean Alps; as he spoke of which there was often a tremulous tenderness in his voice; and sometimes he expatiated on them with all the fire of genius—sometimes would appear scarcely conscious of the topic, though he continued to speak. This subject recalled forcibly to Emily the idea of her father, whose image appeared in every landscape which Valancourt particularized, whose remarks dwelt upon her memory, and whose enthusiasm still glowed in her heart. Her silence at length reminded Valancourt how nearly his conversation approached to the occasion of her grief [her father's death], and he changed the subject, though for one scarcely less affecting to Emily. When he admired the grandeur of the plane-tree, that spread its wide branches over the terrace, and under whose shade they now sat, she remembered how often she had sat thus with St. Aubert [her father], and heard him express the same admiration.

"This was a favorite tree with my dear father," said she: "he used to love to sit under its foliage, with his family about him, in the fine evenings of summer."

Valancourt understood her feelings, and was silent: had she raised her eyes from the ground, she would have seen tears in his. He rose, and leaned on the wall of the terrace; from which in a few moments he returned to his seat; then rose again, and appeared to be greatly agitated; while Emily found her spirits so much depressed, that several of her attempts to renew the conversation were ineffectual. Valancourt again sat down; but was still silent, and trembled. At length he said with a hesitating voice, "This lovely scene I am going to leave!—to leave you—perhaps for ever! These moments may never return! I cannot resolve to neglect, though I scarcely dare to avail myself of them. Let me, however, without offending the delicacy of your sorrow, venture to declare the admiration I must always feel of your goodness—oh! That at some future period I might be permitted to call it love!"

Emily's emotion would not suffer her to reply; and Valancourt, who now ventured to look up, observing her countenance change, expected to see her faint, and made an involuntary effort to support her, which recalled Emily to a sense of her situation, and to an exertion of her spirits. Valancourt did not appear to notice her indisposition, but when he spoke again, his voice told the tenderest love. "I will not presume," he added, "to intrude this subject longer upon your attention at this time; but

I may perhaps be permitted to mention, that these parting
moments would lose much of their bitterness, if I might be
allowed to hope the declaration I have made would not exclude
me from your presence in future."

***

It was now the second watch of the night; and about the
time when the figure had before appeared, Emily heard the
passing footsteps of the sentinels on the rampart, as they
changed guard; and when all was again silent, she took her station at the casement, leaving her lamp in a remote part of the
chamber, that she might escape notice from without. The moon
gave a faint and uncertain light, for heavy vapors surrounded
it, and often rolling over the disk, left the scene below in total
darkness. It was in one of these moments of obscurity that she
observed a small and lambent flame moving at some distance
on the terrace. While she gazed, it disappeared; and the moon
again emerging from the lurid and heavy thunder clouds, she
turned her attention to the heavens, where the vivid lightnings
darted from cloud to cloud, and flashed silently on the woods
below. She loved to catch in the momentary gleam the gloomy
landscape. Sometimes a cloud opened its light upon a distant
mountain; and, while the sudden splendour illumined all its
recess of rock and wood, the rest of the scene remained in
deep shadow; at others, partial features of the castle were
revealed by the glimpse—the ancient arch leading to the east
rampart, the turret above, or the fortifications beyond; and
then, perhaps, the whole edifice, with all its towers, its dark
massy walls and pointed casements, would appear, and vanish
in an instant.

Emily looking up again on the rampart, perceived the
flame she had seen before; it moved onward; and soon after
she thought she heard a footstep. The light appeared and disappeared frequently, while, as she watched, it glided under
her casements, and at the same instant she was certain that a
footstep passed, but the darkness did not permit her to distinguish any object except the flame. It moved away, and then,
by a gleam of lightning, she perceived some person on the terrace. All the anxieties of the preceding night returned. This
person advanced, and the playing flame alternately appeared
and vanished. Emily wished to speak, to end her doubts
whether this figure were human or supernatural; but her cour-
age failed as often as she attempted utterance, till the light
moved again under the casement, and she faintly demanded
who passed. . . .

[It turns out to be one of the castle's young guards and the
light Emily has seen is reflecting off of his lance—but he cannot
explain why. He mentioned a fellow soldier had a similar experience

with a mysterious light reflecting off his weapon and he regarded this phenomenon as an omen.]

Whether Emily was alarmed by this omen, or not, she certainly was relieved from much terror by discovering this man to be only a soldier on duty, and it immediately occurred to her that it might be he who had occasioned so much alarm on the preceding night. There were, however, some circumstances that still required explanation. As far as she could judge by the faint moonlight that had assisted her observation, the figure she had seen did not resemble this man either in shape or size; besides, she was certain it had carried no arms. The silence of its steps, if steps it had, the moaning sounds, too, which it had uttered, and its strange disappearance, were circumstances of mysterious import, that did not apply, with probability, to a soldier engaged in the duty of a guard.

Source: Ann Radcliffe, *The Mysteries of Udolfo*, Everyman's Library (New York: Dutton, 1931), 1:108–109, 2:42–43.

Document 11: Mary Shelley, from *Frankenstein* (1818)

Mary Wollstonecraft Godwin Shelley (1797–1851) had a pedigree that involved intellectual giants of late eighteenth-century England—her mother was Mary Wollstonecraft (1759–1797), whose *Vindication of the Rights of Woman* (1792) passionately argued for better education for women, so that those who married could be interesting companions for their husbands or those who did not could support themselves. Her father, William Godwin (1756–1836), was a radical philosopher, who anguished over the ills of contemporary society and argued that governments should be disbanded in favor of smaller communities, where individuals would not have to conform to institutional (government or church) dictates. Mary's mother died shortly after giving birth to her, and her father quickly remarried. Mary's step-mother was not particularly fond of her and Mary "eloped" with Percy Bysshe Shelley in her mid-teens. While in Switzerland the summer of 1816, in the company of Lord Byron, a group of writers agreed to the challenge of writing a ghost story. Mary's story grew into the novel *Frankenstein*, which was published anonymously two years later.

The themes found in *Frankenstein* parallel those explored by many Romantics, acknowledging individual genius and its quest, the power and awe inspired by nature, a growing interest in scientific research, such as man's desire to understand and harness the powers of nature, and the critical need for family and personal interrelationships. Victor Frankenstein embodies the Romantic ideal of a genius with a mission: he wants to create life from inanimate objects. His success does not bring happiness. Mary Shelley could be saying that in some cases, even with the best intentions, actions can lead to tragic results. She could be attacking male behavior, which can be threatening or destructive to society. Another possibility is that she is criticizing egocentric men, who think they are above the laws of nature and God.[4]

The following selection recounts Victor Frankenstein's trip to the French Alps and his experience of the sublime.

> I performed the first part of my journey on horseback. I afterwards hired a mule, as the more sure-footed and least liable to receive injury on these rugged roads. The weather was fine: it was about the middle of the month of August.... The weight upon my spirit was sensibly lightened as I plunged yet deeper in the ravine of Arve [a valley near Swiss-French border, near Chamonix]. The immense mountains and precipices that overhung me on every side—the sound of the river raging among the rocks, and the dashing of the waterfalls around, spoke of a power mighty as Omnipotence—and I ceased to fear, or to bend before any being less almighty than that which had created and ruled the elements, here displayed in their most terrific guise. Still, as I ascended higher, the valley assumed a more magnificent and astonishing character. Ruined castles hanging on the precipices of piny mountains; the impetuous Arve, and cottages every here and there peeping forth from among the trees, formed a scene of singular beauty. But it was augmented and rendered sublime by the mighty Alps, whose white and shining pyramids and domes towered above all, as belonging to another earth, the habitations of another race of beings.
>
> I passed the bridge of Pélissier, where the ravine, which the river forms, opened before me, and I began to ascend the mountain that overhangs it. Soon after, I entered the valley of Chamounix. This valley is more wonderful and sublime, but not so beautiful and picturesque as that of Servox, through which I had just passed. The high and snowy mountains were its immediate boundaries, but I saw no more ruined castles and fertile fields. Immense glaciers approached the road; I heard their rumbling thunder of the falling avalanche and marked the smoke of its passage. Mont Blanc, the supreme and magnificent Mont Blanc, raised itself from the surrounding *aiguilles* [needle-shaped peaks], and its tremendous dome overlooked the valley.
>
> A tingling long-lost sense of pleasure often came across me during this journey. Some turn in the road, some new object suddenly perceived and recognized, reminded me of days gone

by, and were associated with the light-hearted gaiety of boyhood. The very winds whispered in soothing accents, and maternal Nature bade me weep no more. Then again the kindly influence ceased to act—I found myself fettered again to grief and indulging in all the misery of reflection. Then I spurred on my animal, striving to forget the world, my fears, and more than all, myself—or, in a more desperate fashion, I alighted and threw myself on the grass, weight down by horror and despair.

Source: Mary Shelley, *Frankenstein, or the Modern Prometheus* (New York: E. P. Dutton and Co., 1912), 95–96.

Document 12: Madame de Staël, from *Germany* (1810)

Anne Louise Germaine Necker de Staël-Holstein (1766–1817) was, along with Goethe, considered the most cosmopolitan of the intellectuals who lived and wrote during the Age of Romanticism. Born in to a well-connected family, since her father was the financial advisor to the French king, she frequented literary salons from an early age and, once married, established one herself. She had entered an arranged marriage at age twenty, and took on lovers without too much afterthought. One, writer and politician Benjamin Constant (1767–1830), helped her develop an interest in the German lands. When Napoleon ordered her from France in late 1803, she began her exile with a lengthy tour through Germany. She met the Schlegel brothers and others associated with German Romanticism. She was quite taken by the fact that there was no centralized German government, but rather many small principalities. She felt this lack of a strong central government allowed for more intellectual freedom for artists. In 1810, she secretly returned to Paris to get her manuscript *Germany* published. Authorities discovered it, and Napoleon ordered all extant copies destroyed. It was published in England several years later. In the work, she overstates some qualities about the Germans, at the implied expense of France, so it is no wonder that French authorities, and Napoleon in particular, disliked the book.

> [from Chapter 2, "On the Manners and Character of the Germans"]
> The demarcation of classes, much more positive in Germany than it used to be in France, naturally produced the annihilation of military spirit among the lower orders; this demarcation has in fact nothing offensive in it; for I repeat, a sort of natural goodness mixes itself with every thing in Germany, even with aristocratical pride; and the differences of rank are reduced to some court

privileges, to some assemblies which do not afford sufficient pleasure to deserve envy: nothing is bitter, under whatever aspect contemplated, when society, and ridicule, which is the offspring of society, is without influence. Men cannot really wound their very souls, except by falsehood or mockery: in a country of seriousness and truth, justice and happiness will always be met with. But the barrier which separated, in Germany, the nobles from the citizens, necessarily rendered the whole nation less warlike.

Imagination, which is the ruling quality of the world or arts and letters in Germany, inspires the fear of danger, if this natural emotion is not combated by the ascendancy of opinion and the exaltation of honor. In France, even in its ancient state, the taste for war was universal: and the common people willingly risked life, as a means of agitating it and diminishing the sense of its weight. It is a question of importance to know whether the domestic affections, the habit of reflection, the very gentleness of soul, do not conduce to the fear of death; but if the whole strength of a State consist in its military spirit, it is of consequence to examine what are the causes that have weakened this spirit in the German nation.

Three leading motives usually incite men to fight,—the patriotic love of liberty, the enthusiasm for glory, and religious fanaticism. There can be no great patriotism in an empire divided for so many ages, where Germans fought against Germans, almost always instigated by some foreign impulse: the love of glory is scarcely awake where there is no centre, no society. That species of impartiality, the very excess of justice, which characterizes the Germans, renders them much more susceptible of being inflamed with abstract sentiments, than of the real interests of life; the general who loses a battle, is more sure of indulgence than he who gains one is of applause; there is not enough difference between success and reverse, in the opinions of such a people, to excite any very lively ambition.

[from Chapter 4, "On the Influence of the Spirit of Chivalry on Love and Honor"]

Love is a much more serious quality in Germany than in France. Poetry, the fine arts, even philosophy and religion, have made this sentiment an object of earthly adoration, which sheds a noble charm over life. Germany was not infested, like France, with licentious writings, which circulated among all the classes of people, and effected the destruction of sentiment among the high, and of morality among the low. It must be allowed, nevertheless, that the Germans have more imagination than sensibility; and their uprightness is the only pledge for their constancy. The French, in general, respect positive duties; the Germans think themselves less bound by duty than affection. What we have said respecting the facility of divorce affords a proof of this;

love is, with them, more sacred than marriage. It is the effect of an honorable delicacy, no doubt, that they are above all things faithful to promises which the law does not warrant; but those which are warranted by law are nevertheless of greater importance to the interest of society.

Source: Madame the Baroness de Staël-Holstein, *Germany*, vol. 1, with notes and appendices by O. W. Wight (New York: Derby and Jackson, 1860), 39–40, 51.

Document 13: Victor Hugo, from his preface to *Cromwell* (1827)

Victor Hugo (1802–1885) aspired to be a writer and idolized the Vicomte de Chateaubriand. Through a very long life, Hugo wrote poems, dramas, and novels, which embodied Romantic values. The "Preface" to his drama *Cromwell* placed him directly in the Romantic tradition. In it, he discusses the sweep of Western Civilization often using the theater as his leitmotiv. He suggests civilization has passed from infancy, middle age and is now in its old age. Such change necessitates new approaches to art and artistic production. He expounds on his views about how contemporary dramas should be produced, in part to attack the Classical tradition in drama of the three unities: time, place, and action. It is really not a profound theoretical treatise, but it invites new thinking about the possibilities for stage productions.

In the section that follows, Hugo discusses the relationship between nature and art. He also suggests that dramas should explore "local color."

> We must admit, therefore, or confess ourselves ridiculous, that the domains of art and of nature are entirely distinct. Nature and art are two things—were it not so, one or the other would not exist. Art, in addition to its idealistic side, has a terrestrial, material side. Let it do what it will, it is shut in between grammar and prosody, between Vaugelas and Richelet.[5] For its most capricious creations, it has formulæ, methods of execution, a complete apparatus to set in motion. For genius there are delicate instruments, for mediocrity, tools.
>
> It seems to us that someone has already said that the drama is a mirror wherein nature is reflected. But if it be an ordinary mirror, a smooth and polished surface, it will give only a dull image of objects, with no relief—faithful, but colourless; everyone knows that colour and light are lost in a simple reflection. The drama, therefore, must be a concentrating

mirror, which, instead of weakening, concentrates and con-
denses the coloured rays, which makes of a mere gleam a
light, and of a light a flame. Then only is the drama acknowledged by art.

The stage is an optical point. Everything that exists in the
world—in history, in life, in man—should be and can be
reflected therein, but under the magic wand of art. Art turns the
leaves of the ages, of nature, studies chronicles, strives to reproduce actual facts (especially in respect to manners and peculiar-
ities, which are much less exposed to doubt and contradictions
than are concrete facts), restores what the chroniclers have
lopped off, harmonises what they have collected, divines and
supplies their omissions, fills their gaps with imaginary scenes
which have the colour of the time, groups what they have left
scattered about, sets in motion anew the threads of Providence
which work the human marionettes, clothes the whole with a
form at once poetical and natural, and imparts to it that vitality
of truth and brilliancy which gives birth to illusion, that prestige
of reality which arouses the enthusiasm of the spectator, and of
the poet first of all, for the poet is sincere. Thus the aim of art
is almost divine: to bring to life again if it is writing history, to
create if it is writing poetry.

It is a grand and beautiful sight to see this broad development of a drama wherein art powerfully seconds nature; of a
drama wherein the plot moves on to the conclusion with a firm
and unembarrassed step, without diffuseness and without undue
compression; of a drama, in short, wherein the poet abundantly
fulfills the multifold object of art, which is to open to the spectator a double prospect, to illuminate at the same time the interior and the exterior of mankind: the exterior by their speech
and their acts, the interior, by asides and monologues; to bring
together, in a work in the same picture, the drama of life and
the drama of conscience.

It will readily be imagined that, for a work of this kind, if
the poet must *choose* (and he must), he should choose, not the
beautiful, but the *characteristic*. Not that it is advisable to "make
local colour," as they say to-day; that is, to add as an afterthought a few discordant touches here and there to a work that
is at best utterly conventional and false. The local colour should
not be on the surface of the drama, but in its substance, in the
very heart of the work, whence it spreads of itself, naturally,
evenly, and, so to speak, into every corner of the drama, as the
sap ascends from the root to the tree's topmost leaf. The drama
should be thoroughly impregnated with this colour of the time,
which should be, in some sort, in the air, so that one detects it
only on entering the theatre, and that on going forth one finds
one's self in a different period and atmosphere. It requires some
study, some labour, to attain this end; so much the better. It is

well that the avenues of art should be obstructed by those brambles from which everybody recoils except those of powerful will. Besides, it is this very study, fostered by an ardent inspiration, which will ensure the drama against a vice that kills it—the *commonplace*. To be commonplace is the failing of short-sighted, short-breathed poets. In this tableau of the stage, each figure must be held down to its most prominent, most individual, most precisely defined characteristic. Even the vulgar and the trivial should have an accent of their own. Like God, the true poet is present in every part of his work at once. Genius resembles the die which stamps the king's effigy on copper and golden coins alike.

Source: Victor Hugo, "Preface to Cromwell," in *Prefaces and Prologues to Famous Books*, Harvard Classics, vol. 39 (New York: P. F. Collier and Son, 1910), 386–388.

Document 14: Alessandro Manzoni, from *The Betrothed* (1827)

Alessandro Manzoni (1785–1873) settled in Milan in 1810 after having spent five years in Paris where he frequented the liberal salon of Madame de Condorcet. He resided in Milan for the remainder of his life; the only recorded trip was to Tuscany in the late 1820s to study the local dialect. He began work on *I Promessi Sposi* (*The Betrothed*) in 1821 and completed it four years later. After undertaking linguistic studies, he decided that the Tuscan dialect should become the literary language of Italy and rewrote the entire novel in Tuscan.

The story takes place between 1628 and 1630, when Spanish overlords dominated Milan and the War of Mantuan Succession (1628–1630) disrupted people's lives. Against the backdrop of foreign nobles controlling society, the outbreak of the plague, and constant warfare, the story of two peasants plays out. They wish to marry, but the wicked Don Rodrigo has other ideas. In the same vein as Sir Walter Scott, who praised the novel as a great romance, the realistic descriptions of the regions in and around Milan serve as the background to this story of love, deception, and pride. The selection that follows reveals Manzoni's affinity with other Romantic writers in his descriptions of landscapes and allusions to mysterious castles and evil people. Don Rodrigo travels to the foreboding castle to seek the help of the unscrupulous noble (the Unnamed) to gain access to the young peasant girl Lucia, who had sought refuge in a convent.

Don Rodrigo liked well enough to play the tyrant, but not the fierce and savage tyrant: the profession was to him a means, not an end: he wished to live at freedom in the city, to enjoy the convenience, diversions, and honours of social life; and for the end he was obliged to keep up a certain appearance, make much of his family, cultivate the friendship of persons in place. . . .

One morning, Don Roderigo set off on horseback, in the guise of a hunter, with a small escort of bravoes on foot, Griso at his side, and four others following behind him, and took the road to the castle of the Unnamed.

Chapter XX

The castle of the Unnamed was commandingly situated over a dark and narrow valley, on the summit of a cliff projecting from a rugged ridge of hills, whether united to them or separated from them it is difficult to say, by a mass of crags and rocks, and by a boundary of caverns and abrupt precipices, both flanking it and on the rear. The side which overlooked the valley was the only accessible one; rather a steep acclivity, certainly, but even and unbroken: the summit was used for pasturage, while the lower grounds were cultivated, and scattered here and there with habitations. . . .

From the height of this castle, like an eagle from his sanguinary nest, the savage nobleman surveyed every spot around where the foot of man could tread, and heard no human sound above him. At one view he could overlook the whole vale, the declivities, the bed of the stream, and the practicable paths intersecting the valley. That which approached his terrible abode by a zigzag and serpentine course appeared to the spectator from below like a winding thread; while from the windows and loopholes on the summit, the Signor could leisurely observe any one who was ascending, and a hundred times catch a view of him. With the garrison of bravoes whom he there maintained, he could even oppose a tolerably numerous troop of assailants, stretching any number of them on the ground, or hurling them to the bottom, before they could succeed in gaining the height.

Source: Alessandro Manzoni, *I Promessi Sposi* (*The Betrothed*), Harvard Classics, vol. 21 (New York: P. F. Collier and Son, 1909), 331–333.

Document 15: Caspar David Friedrich, from his diary (1803)

As with many Romantic artists, Caspar David Friedrich (1774–1840) enjoyed outdoor hikes and found in them not only a way to relax but a means to find inspiration from nature. In the following diary entry, he recounts viewing the Elster River Valley and a visit to Elsterwerde, a town in the southern part of Brandenburg. Today, a park called the *Niederlausitzer Heidelandschaft* (Niederlausitz Moorland) surrounds the city, which is a tourist destination with its bike paths and pleasant landscapes. Friedrich's description of the landscape and its sights conveys the Romantics' appreciation for nature and how it inspired them.

> I stepped out of a dark forest and found myself on a precipice. Before me in a valley surrounded by fertile hillsides lay a lovely town and in the twilight the new roof of the slate tower sparkled. The Elster River snaked through the flower-filled meadow and it was a beautiful sight. Behind the hills lay the mountains and behind the mountains the great cliffs loomed, so each great rock lay atop one another, reaching into the lofty distance. Full of total joy I stood there a while and looked around the beautiful area and saw the herds of cows and sheep near the little town and how the hard-working reapers with their glittering scythes hurried back to Elsterwerda. I became mindful of the beautiful young girls, who I had seen a few months earlier when I had passed through the area. I hurried before it got dark to get to town. Slowly I walked through the quiet narrow streets and saw a few beautiful young girls; it was the same ones whom I had previously seen. Gazing through a clear window, I barely had time to give them a friendly nod, than they quickly turned away blushing profusely.
>
> Soft rising hills obstructed the distant view, at the same time the children's wishes, they enjoy the precious present moment only by wanting what lies beyond. Burning bushes, nourishing herbs, fragrant flowers surround the still clear stream, in which the pure blue of the clear sky reflects, as in children's souls—God's beautiful images, children play, kissing and enjoying themselves and one child greets the coming sun with happy clapping, Lambs graze in the valley and on the hills. No stone can be seen, no barren branches or fallen leaves. All nature breathes peace, joy and innocence and life.
>
> You know my apartment and its beautiful view. Today for the first time, this region reminded me of the past and death, when usually it inspires a sense of joy and life. The heavens are dark and stormy and for the first time the beautiful colorful mountains and field are covered with a monochrome blanket of snow. Pale nature lies before me.

Source: Caspar David Friedrich, *Caspar David Friedrich in Briefen and Bekenntnissen*, ed. Sigrid Hinz (Berlin: Henschelverlag Kunst und Gesellschaft, 1968), 81 (translated by Joanne Schneider). Used by permission of Seemann Henschel GmbH and Co., KG.

Document 16: Ludwig van Beethoven, letters to Countess Giulietta Guicciardi and Goethe (1801 and 1811)

Ludwig van Beethoven (1770–1827) stands as a luminary in the history of Western music. He serves as the touchstone for modern music and the inspiration for great orchestral sounds that came after him. Beethoven's letters provide insight into his thoughts, cares, and personal relationships. After Beethoven established residence in Vienna in 1792, he developed a circle of friends and patrons as he gave concerts and his reputation grew. In 1803 or 1804, he began giving music lessons to Archduke Rudolph (1788–1831), the youngest son of Emperor Leopold II (ruled 1790–1792). The young archduke was apparently a motivated student. The two remained close and Beethoven dedicated many works to Rudolph, including the *Missa solemnis*.

Beethoven did not hold an official music position at the Viennese court, rather he supported himself, in part, through periodic stipends patrons gave him. Such generosity allowed him to devote his efforts to composing. The wars against Napoleon did make life in Vienna unsettling and Beethoven threatened to relocate. At this time, Archduke Rudolph and two other nobles, Prince Lobkowitz and Prince Ferdinand Kinsky, agreed to provide Beethoven with a generous yearly allowance for life.[6]

The first selection is regarded as one of Beethoven's most wonderful letters. It is addressed to his "Immortal Beloved" Giulietta Guicciardi (1784–1856), who had started piano lessons with Beethoven in 1801. He fell in love and wanted to marry her, but her father disapproved of the match, in part because of Beethoven's inferior social status. The second selection reveals Beethoven humbled by another great of his time, Goethe. Beethoven has written music to accompany Goethe's drama *Egmont*, and asks him to comment on that effort.

> To Countess Giulietta Guicciardi
> On the 6th of July [1801?] in the morning.
> My Angel, My All, My Very Self,
> Just a few words to-day, and only in pencil—(with thine) only till to-morrow is my room definitely engaged, what an unworthy waste of time in such matters—why this deep sorrow where necessity speaks. Can our love endure otherwise than through sacrifices, through restraint in longing. Canst thou help

not being wholly mine, can I, not being wholly thine. Oh! Gaze at nature in all its beauty, and calmly accept the inevitable—love demands everything, and rightly so. *Thus is it for me with thee, for thee with me,* only thou so easily forgettest, that I must live for myself and for thee—were we wholly united thou wouldst feel this painful fact as little as I should—my journey was terrible. I arrived here only yesterday morning at four o'clock and as they were short of horses, the mail-coach selected another route, but what an awful road; at the last stage but one I was warned against traveling by night; they frightened me with the wood, but that only spurred me on—and I was wrong, the coach must needs breakdown, the road being dreadful, a swamp, a mere country road; without the postilions [riders accompanying his coach] I had with me, I should have stuck on the way. Esterhazi, by ordinary road, met the same fate with eight horses as I with four—yet it gave me some pleasure, as successfully overcoming any difficulty always does. Now for a quick change from without to within: we shall probably soon see each other, besides, to-day I cannot tell thee what has been passing through my mind during the past few days concerning my life—were our hearts closely united, I should not do things of this kind. My heart is full of the many things I have to say to thee—ah!—there are moments in which I feel that speech is powerless—cheer up—remain my true my only treasure, my all!!! as I to thee. The gods must send the rest, what for us must be and ought to be.

Thy faithful,
Ludwig

Monday evening, July 6

Thou sufferest, thou my dearest love. I have just found out that the letters must be posted very early Mondays, Thursdays—the only days when the post goes from here to K. Thou sufferest—Ah! where I am, art thou also with me; I will arrange for myself and Thee. I will manage so that I can live with thee; and what a life!!!! But as it is!!!! without thee. Persecuted here and there by the kindness of men, which I little deserve, and as little care to deserve. Humility of man towards man—it pains me—and when I think of myself in connection with the universe, what am I and what is He who is named the Greatest: and still this again shows the divine in man. I weep when I think that probably thou wilt only get the first news from me on Saturday evening. However, much thou lovest me, my love for thee is stronger, but never conceal thy thoughts from me. Good-night. As I am taking the baths I must go to bed [two words, scratched through]. O God—so near! So far! Our, love is it not a true heavenly edifice, firm as heaven's vault.

Good morning on July 7

While still in bed, my thoughts press to thee, my Beloved One, at moments with joy, and then again with sorrow, waiting to see whether fate will take pity on us. Either I must live wholly with thee or not at all. Yes, I have resolved to wander in distant lands, until I can fly to thy arms, and feel that with thee I have a real home with thee encircling me about, I can send my soul into the kingdom of spirits. Yes, unfortunately, it must be so. Calm thyself, and all the more since thou knowest my faithfulness towards thee, never can another possess my heart, never—never—O God, why must one part from what one so loves, and yet my life in V. at present is a wretched life. Thy love has made me one of the happiest and, at the same time, one of the unhappiest of men—at my age I need a quiet, steady life—is that possible in our situation? My Angel, I have just heard that the post goes every day, and I must therefore stop, so that you may receive the letter without delay. Be calm, only by calm consideration of our existence can we attain our aim to live together—be calm—love me—to-day—yesterday—what tearful longing after thee—thee—thee—my life—my all—farewell—Oh, continue to love me—never misjudge the faithful heart

Of thy Beloved

L

ever thine

ever mine

ever each other's

To Herr Von Goethe Excellenz

Vienna, April 12, 1811

Your Excellency!

The pressing opportunity of a friend of mine, one of your great admirers (as I also am), who is leaving here in a great hurry, gives me only a moment to offer my thanks for the long time I have known you (for I know you from the days of my childhood)—that is very little for so much. Bettine Brentano [a mutual friend of Beethoven's and Goethe's] has assured me that you would receive me in kindly, yes, indeed, friendly spirit. But how could I think of such a reception, seeing that I am only in a position to approach you with the deepest reverence, with an inexpressibly deep feeling for your noble creations. You will shortly receive from Leipzig through Breitkopf and Härtel the music to *Egmont*, this Glorious *Egmont*, with which I, with the same warmth with which I read it, was again through you impressed by it, and set it to music. I should much like to know your opinion of it; even blame will be profitable for me and for my art, and will be as willingly received as the greatest praise.

Your Excellency's great admirer,
Ludwig van Beethoven

Source: Ludwig van Beethoven, *Beethoven's Letters, with Explanatory Notes by Dr. A. C. Kalischer*, trans. J. S. Shedlock (New York: E. P. Dutton and Co., 1926), 31–33, 114.

Document 17: Johann Wolfgang von Goethe, from *The Italian Journey* (1816)

After the publication of *The Sorrows of Young Werther*, Goethe was invited to visit Charles Augustus, Duke of Saxe-Weimar (1757–1828) in Weimar. As a result, Goethe accepted a ministerial position, which he held for ten years. He fit in well with the local aristocratic set and also fell in love with a slightly older married woman, Charlotte von Stein (1742–1827). In part to overcome that intense but unconsummated relationship and to escape his boring job, he left Weimar for a sojourn in Italy, which lasted from 1786 to 1788. The letters he wrote and the diaries he kept from that journey were eventually published in 1816 as *Die italienische Reise* (*The Italian Journey*). Its descriptions of the Italian landscapes reflect the Romantic fascination with nature and its beauties. It also contained observations about local rock formations and the like—which made it fascinating for the Romantics, because it was a diverse document, part memoir, part travelogue, part scientific observation, and part comment on local society. Goethe returned to Weimar, where he spent the rest of his life. He continued writing and also served as the director of the local theater and scientific society.

Rome
19 February 1787
The weather for all appearances continues to remain beautiful.... The new moon has passed and next to its delicate sliver, unassisted I could almost see the entire dark orb—which I could clearly see with a telescope. A haze hovered over the earth all day, that one only recognizes from Claude's [Claude Lorraine, 1600–1682] paintings and sketches—the phenomena of nature, that is not so easy to see unless one is here. Flowers that I do not recognize are blooming as well as buds on trees; the blossoming almond trees create an airy appearance between the dark green oaks; the sky is like bright blue taffeta illuminated by the sun. I wonder what it would look like in Naples? Everything [here] is already green. My botanical fancy increases through all of this; I am in the process of discovering new, beautiful

situations where nature develops something so overwhelming
out of what looks like so little. . . .

Mt. Vesuvius is currently throwing out stones and ashes
and at night its peak glows. If only nature would give us a river
of lava! I can hardly expect that this idea is unique to me.

Source: Johann Wolfgang von Goethe, *Goethe's Italienische Reise*, ed.
Kurt Jahn (Leipzig: Insel-Verlag, 1930), 183 (translated by Joanne
Schneider).

Document 18: John Clare, from *Sketches in the Life of John Clare* (1821)

John Clare (1793–1864), his life, and works illustrate the ecological awareness that was common to some Romantics. While many
of them found intellectual inspiration in nature, he not only did that,
but he also labored in the fields of his native Northamptonshire. He
witnessed how enclosure was changing the lives of peasant farmers,
the local topography, and the economy. Having virtually no formal
schooling, he began work at age seven and read what and when he
could. He published his first poetry collection *Poems Descriptive of
Rural Life and Scenery* in 1820. He traveled to London and became
the toast of high society. He received a stipend from a wealthy patron
and returned home to continue writing, but the demands of a large
family and the mediocre reception of his second poetry volume left
him in dire financial straits. He was forced to resort to day labor to
support his family. He also started drinking. After his book *The Rural
Muse* (1835) appeared and was virtually ignored, he fell into para-
noia. He was placed in an asylum from which he escaped in 1841.
He spent about half a year with his family, but at the end of 1841,
he was declared insane and spent the rest of his life institutionalized.

Clare prided himself on using the language of the local people,
against the wishes of his editors in London who were always trying
to elevate his poetry to standard English. He resented the tampering
with his works. After his first volume of poetry was published, Clare
wrote *Sketches in the Life of John Clare* (1821). This autobiographical
sketch introduces the world of rural central England and the village
and countryside in which Clare lived and worked. The following
selections discuss his purchase of a copy of K. Thomson's *Seasons*
when he was thirteen, which inspired him to become a poet, and
how looking over the landscape led him to begin his first major
work, and later how he hid his poems from his parents.

I started off, and as we was generally soon [early] with getting out our horses, that they might fill themselves before the flies was out, I got to Stamford, I dare say, before a door had been opened, and loitered about the town for hours ere I could obtain my wishes. I at length got it, [the Thompson book] with an agreeable disappointment in return for my first, buying it for 6d. [pence] less than I propos'd, and never was I more pleased with a bargain than I was with this shilling purchase. [He has origi- nally been told the book would cost him one shilling six pence.] On my return the sun got up, and it was a beautiful morning; I could not wait till I got back without reading it, and as I did not like to let anybody see me reading on the road of a working day, I clumb over the wall in to Burghley Park, and nestled in a lawn at the wall side.

The Scenery around me was uncommonly beautiful at that time of the year, and what with reading the book, and beholding the beauties of artful nature in the park, I got into a strain of de- scriptive rhyming on my journey home. This was "The Morning Walk," the first thing I committed to paper. I afterwards wrote the "Evening Walk," and several descriptions of Local Spots in the fields, which I had frequented for pootys, flowers, or nests in my early childhood. I burned most of these after I got to con- ceit I knew better how to make poetry; others I corrected per- haps 20 times over till their original form was entirely lost. Such is the "Morning Walk" now extant. . . .

***

I now ventured to commit my musings readily to paper, but with all secrecy possible, hiding them when written in an old unused cupboard in the chamber which when taken for other purpose drove me to the necessity of seeking another safety in a hole under it in the wall. Here my mother when cleaning the chamber found me out, and secretly took my papers for her own use as occasion call'd for them: [she used them to kindle her cooking fire]; and as I had no other desire in me but to keep them from being read, when laid in this fancied safe repository, that desire seem'd compleated, and I rarely turned to a reperusal [reread] of them. Consequently my stolen fugitives went a long time ere they was miss'd; my mother thought they was nothing more than Copies, as attempts at improving myself in writing. She knew nothing of poetry, at least little dreamed her son was employed in that business; and as I was ashamed of being found out as an attempter in that way, when I discovered the thefts, I hum- oured her mistake a long time, and said they was nothing more than what she supposed them to be; so she might take them, but when I did things that I liked better than others, I provided safer lodgings for them.

At length I began to shake off this reserve with my parents, and half confess what I was doing. My father would sometimes be humming over a song, a wretched composition of those halfpenny ballads, and my boast was that I thought I could beat it; in a few days afterward I used to read my composition for his judgment to decide; but their frequent criticism and laughable remarks drove me to use a process of cunning in the business—some time after, for they damp'd me a long time from proceeding.

My method on resuming the matter again was to say I had written it out of a borrowed book, and that it was not my own. The love of rhyming which I was loathe to quit, growing fonder of it every day, drove me to the necessity of a lie to try the value of their criticisms, and by the way I got their remarks unadulterated with prejudice. . . .

Source: John Clare, *Sketches in the Life of John Clare Written by Himself*, intro. Edmund Blunden (London: Cobden-Sanderson, 1931), 59–60, 61–63.

Document 19: Dorothy Wordsworth, from "Of a Tour on the Continent" (1820)

Dorothy Wordsworth (1771–1855) made several trips with William around the British Isles as well as to Europe. Some of her most memorable prose comes from her journals, where she recounts what they had seen and experienced. The following comes from a tour the Wordsworths made of Switzerland in 1820 and reveals her appreciation of nature, especially a mountain rainstorm, but she also notices the people they met and little things like their folk art household items.

Grindlewald, Friday, August 11th.—Scheideck to Meiringen.—To our right, looking over the green cradle of the vale, we saw the glacier, with the stream issuing from beneath an arch of solid ice—the small pyramids around it of a grayish colour, mingled with vitriol green. The bed of icy snow above looked sullied, so that the glacier itself was not beautiful, like what we had read of; but the mass of mountains behind, their black crags and shadows, and the awful aspect of winter encroaching on the valley-domain (combinations so new to us) made ample amends for any disappointment we might feel. . . . The rain came on in heavy drops, but did not drive us to the closer shelter of the house. We heeded not the sprinkling which a gust of wind sometimes sent in upon us. Good fortune had hitherto favoured us; and, even if we had been detained at that house all night, the inconvenience would have been trifling. Our spirits were uplifted, and we felt as if it would be a privilege to be admitted to a near acquaintance with Alpine storms. This at least was my feeling, till the threatenings were over; and then, by happy transition, I gladly hailed the bursting light of the sun that flashed upon the crags, seen by glimpses between the dispersing clouds. The interior of the house was roomy and warm and, though the floors were of the bare soil, everything looked cleanly; the wooden vessels were pretty, ladles and spoons curiously carved, and neatly arranged on shelves. Three generations, making a numerous family, were there living together in the summer season, with their cattle on the rough pastures round them: no doubt the main support of the household, but the gains from travelers must be considerable. We were surprised at being asked if we chose coffee. Hardly should we have deserved our welcome shelter had we not preferred the peasant's fare—cheese, milk, and cream, with the addition of bread fetched from the vale; and I must not omit a dish of fruit—bilberries—here very fine. Indeed most of our mountain plants, except the branchy fern and the common daisy (which we rarely saw), grow in lavish beauty, and many others unknown to us, that enamel the tuft like gems. . . .

The storm over, we proceeded, still in the forest, which led us through different compartments of the vale, each of itself a little valley of the loveliest greenness, on all side skirted with pine-trees, and often sprinkled with huts, the summer dwellings of the herdsmen. . . .

Source: Dorothy Wordsworth, *Journals of Dorothy Wordsworth*, vol. 2, ed. William Knight (New York: Macmillan, 1897), 207–208.

Notes

1. A more modern translation of these sentences reads: "It will be objected that we had in the end a relationship of a different character. I agree. But wait, I cannot tell everything at the same time." Jean Jacques Rousseau, *The Confessions*, trans. J. M. Cohen (Baltimore: Penguin Books, 1954), 107.

2. Another modern difference: "How often have I kissed *my* bed because she had slept in it; my curtains, all the furniture of my room, since they belonged to her and her fair hand had touched them; even the floor on to which I threw myself, calling to mind how she had walked there!" Ibid., 108.

3. See Anne K. Mellor, *Romanticism and Gender* (New York: Routledge, 1993), 91–93.

4. See Stephen Behrendt, "Mary Shelley's *Frankenstein* and the Woman Writer's Fate," in *Romantic Women Writers*, ed. Paula R. Feldman and Theresa M. Kelley (Hanover, NH: University Press of New England, 1995), 71–72; Aidan Day, *Romanticism* (New York: Routledge, 1996), 162–163; and David Morse, *Romanticism: A Structural Analysis* (Totowa, NJ: Barnes and Noble, 1982), 82.

5. Claude Favre of Vaugelas (1585–1650), grammarian and author of the French Academy's dictionary of the French language, published in 1653; and Pierre Richelet (1631–1694), who produced the first monolingual French dictionary in hopes of standardizing the language in 1680.

6. The contract that Beethoven signed with the three men in 1809 can be found in *Beethoven's Letters, Journals, and Conversations*, ed. and trans. Michael Hamburger (New York: Thames and Hudson, 1984), 72–74.

ANNOTATED BIBLIOGRAPHY

Primary Sources

Literary Works

An Anthology of Russian Women's Writing, 1777–1992. Edited by Catriona Kelly. New York: Oxford University Press, 1994. A systematic collection of Russian women writers from the past two hundred years, including works by women writing during the Age of Romanticism.

The Ardis Anthology of Russian Romanticism. Edited by Christine Rydel. Ann Arbor, MI: Ardis, 1984. This book is divided according to genre, with an introduction to each. Examples of the principal literary works follow.

Barbauld, Anna Letitia. *The Poems of Anna Letitia Barbauld.* Edited by William McCarthy and Elizabeth Kraft. Athens: University of Georgia Press, 1994. This introduces Barbauld's poems to the modern audience and provides a detailed chronology of her life.

Blake, William. *Blake's Poetry and Designs.* Edited by Mary Lynn Johnson and John E. Grant. New York: W. W. Norton, 1980. This work presents most of Blake's published and unpublished poems, short essays, select letters, and reproductions of the engravings that accompanied many of the poems. It contains essays by six of Blake's contemporaries and ten twentieth-century authors and literary critics.

Byron, George Gordon, Lord. *Byron's Poetry.* Edited by Frank D. McConnell. New York: W. W. Norton, 1978. This collection includes Byron's most well-known poems, selected letters, and entries from his journals. It continues with nine essays of literary and historical criticism. It concludes with commentaries written by his contemporaries and by well-known literary figures of the late nineteenth and early twentieth centuries.

Coleridge, Samuel Taylor. *Coleridge's Poetry and Prose*. Edited by Nicholas Halmi, Paul Magnuson, and Raimonda Modiano. New York: W. W. Norton, 2003. This user-friendly volume contains examples of Coleridge's poetry and philosophical writings. It has extensive explanatory footnotes of his works. It includes twenty essays of literary and historical criticism.

Friedrich Hölderlin: Poems and Fragments. Translated by Michael Hamburger. Ann Arbor: University of Michigan Press, 1967. In addition to a short biography, this work contains Hölderlin's poems in German and in English translation.

Hemans, Felicia. *The Poetical Works of Mrs. Felicia Hemans, Complete in One Volume*. Philadelphia: Porter and Coates, 1853. Mrs. L. H. Sigourney's Victorian-era commentary introduces all of Hemans's known poetry.

Hoffmann, E. T. A. *The Best Tales of Hoffmann*. New York: Dover, 1967. This collection includes ten of his tales. E. F. Bleiler provides a thoughtful introduction to Hoffmann and his life.

Keats, John. *Complete Works of John Keats*. 5 vols. Edited by H. Buxton Forman. New York: AMS Press, 1970. This reissue of a 1900-1901 work purports to contain all of Keats's writings: three volumes of poetry and two of letters.

The Portable Romantic Poets. Edited by W. H. Auden and Normal Holmes Pearson. New York: Viking, 1977. This is a compact collection of the most noted Romantic poets on both sides of the Atlantic, which also contains brief biographies.

Pushkin, Aleksandr Sergeyevitch. *The Complete Prose Tales of Aleksandr Sergeyevitch Pushkin*. Translated by Gillon R. Aitken. New York: W. W. Norton, 1966. The book begins with a brief biographical sketch and then ten tales. Explanatory footnotes accompany each tale.

Rousseau, Jean-Jacques. *Julie, or, The New Heloise: Letters of Two Lovers Who Live in a Small Town at the Foot of the Alps*. Translated and annotated by Philip Stewart and Jean Vaché. Hanover, NH: University Press of New England, 1997. This new translation includes a useful introduction and annotations which explore Rousseau's philosophy.

———. *Rousseau's Political Writings*. Edited by Alan Ritter and Julia Conaway Bondanella. New York: W. W. Norton, 1987. This book includes modern translations of the two discourses and the *Social Contract*. The volume contains contemporary intellectuals' reactions to Rousseau and seven twentieth-century critics' assessments.

Shelley, Mary. *Frankenstein*. Edited by J. Paul Hunter. New York: W. W. Norton, 1995. In addition to the 1818 version of *Frankenstein,* this work contains comments by fellow Romantics such as Percy Bysshe Shelley and Lord Byron and other contemporaries as well as twelve essays by twentieth-century authors.

Shelley, Percy Bysshe. *Shelley's Poetry and Prose*. Edited by Donald H. Reiman and Sharon B. Powers. New York: W. W. Norton, 1977. This volume contains Shelley's most well-known poetry and three prose essays. The primary sources contain extensive explanatory footnotes. It offers four essays of general criticism and then eleven essays that focus on particular works.

Women Romantics, 1785–1832: Writing in Prose. Edited by Jennifer Breen. Rutland, VT: Charles E. Tuttle/Everyman Paperbacks, 1996. This collection includes a general overview of women writers who wrote nonfiction. It also contains brief biographical sketches.

Women's Writing, 1778–1838: An Anthology. Edited by Fiona Robertson. Oxford World Classics. New York: Oxford University Press, 2001. This contains selections from British women authors associated with the Age of Romanticism, including poetry, segments from plays, and nonfiction, and short biographies as well.

Wordsworth, William. *The Prelude, 1799, 1805, 1850*. Edited by Jonathan Wordsworth, M. H. Abrams, and Stephen Gill. New York: W. W. Norton, 1979. This work includes three versions of *The Prelude* and examples of various manuscript drafts. It contains sixteen reviews of the work by various nineteenth-century literary figures. It concludes with seven essays by contemporary scholars who discuss the poem and its meaning.

Memoirs, Letters, and Other Documents

Beethoven's Letters, Journals, and Conversations. Edited, translated, and introduced by Michael Hamburger. New York: Thames and Hudson, 1984. The book includes a brief historical introduction, then a chronology of Beethoven's life and then the collections of various letters, journal entries, and other sources.

Berlioz, Hector. *Memoirs of Hector Berlioz from 1803 to 1865 Comprising Travels in Germany, Italy, Russia, and England*. Translated by Rachel (Scott Russell) Holmes and Eleanor Holmes. Annotated and translation revised by Ernest Newman. New York: Dover, 1966. This colorful memoir provides insight into this gifted musician, who had an interesting sense of humor.

The Death of Franz Liszt Based on the Unpublished Diary of His Pupil Lina Schmalhausen. Edited and introduced by Alan Walker. Ithaca, NY: Cornell University Press, 2002. This work relates the last weeks of Liszt's life and also adds insight into his relationship with Richard Wagner.

Keats, John. *Selected Letters of John Keats*. Revised edition. Based on the texts of Edward Rollins. Edited by Grant T. Scott. Cambridge, MA: Harvard University Press, 2002. This collection shows how Keats took letter writing to the level of art, revealing his spontaneity and intimacy with friends and family and insights about his poetry.

The Letters of John Clare. Edited by J. W. and Anne Tibble. London: Routledge and Kegan Paul, 1951. This work contains not only letters, but also poetry and biographical materials.

Staël, Germaine de. *Ten Years in Exile.* DeKalb: Northern Illinois University Press, 2000. This work includes the two parts of her memoir along with an appendix written by her son and also explanations about her "coded" messages in the text.

Secondary Sources

General Works

Abrams, M. H. *Natural Supernaturalism: Tradition and Revolution in Romantic Literature.* New York: W. W. Norton, 1971. An older but classic investigation of key German and English Romantics and the common traits in their thinking and writing.

Beiser, Frederick. *The Romantic Imperative: The Concept of Early German Romanticism.* Cambridge, MA: Harvard University Press, 2004. This work explores German Romanticism from the perspectives of philosophy, religion, and politics, as well as literature, and revisits Romanticism's importance to today.

Berlin, Isaiah. *The Roots of Romanticism.* The A. W. Mellon Lectures in the Fine Arts, National Gallery of Art, Washington, DC. Bollingen Series XXXV: 45. Princeton, NJ: Princeton University Press, 1999. A lecture given in 1965, where Professor Berlin articulates his reasons for stating that Romanticism as an intellectual movement has affected everything that has subsequently happened in Western culture.

Brookner, Anita. *Romanticism and Its Discontents.* New York: Viking, 2000. A study of French Romanticism that uses as its reference dates 1800 to 1880 and discusses literature and painting from the perspective of the various artists' loss of idealism in the wake of the tumult of the French Revolution and the Age of Napoleon.

Butler, Marilyn. *Romantics, Rebels, and Revolutionaries: English Literature and Its Background, 1760–1830.* Oxford: Oxford University Press, 1982. This important investigation explores the historical context of English Romanticism.

Connell, Philip. *Romanticism, Economics, and the "Question of Culture."* New York: Oxford University Press, 2001. Through literary and intellectual historical approaches, the work investigates the evolving relationship between well-known British Romantic figures and the emergence of the "political economy."

Cranston, Maurice. *The Romantic Movement*. Cambridge, MA: Blackwell, 1994. An introduction to the Romanticism in Europe, which discusses the main figures and their ideas. This work provides an excellent overview for the nonspecialist.

Curran, Stuart, ed. *The Cambridge Companion to British Romanticism*. New York: Cambridge University Press, 1993. Although this anthology focuses on Britain, two of the eleven essays examine Romanticism's relationship to the Enlightenment and German idealist philosophy.

Davis, Leith, ed. *Scotland and the Borders of Romanticism*. Cambridge: Cambridge University Press, 2004. A collection of essays about Scottish literature from 1745 to 1830 and the relationship between the Scottish Enlightenment and British Romanticism. Sir Walter Scott and Joanna Baillie appear in the essays.

Day, Aidan. *Romanticism*. New York: Routledge, 1996. A succinct general introduction to the movement and its primary texts, which addresses the relationship between the Enlightenment and Romanticism.

Duncan, Bruce. *Lovers, Parricides, and Highwaymen: Aspects of the Sturm und Drang*. Rochester, NY: Camden, 1999. An accessible treatment of the *Sturm und Drang*, its writers, and their works. In addition to Goethe and Schiller, German authors less well-known to the English-speaking public are discussed.

Eldridge, Richard, and Robert B. Pippin, eds. *Persistence of Romanticism: Essays in Philosophy and Literature*. Cambridge: Cambridge University Press, 2001. A collection of essays about early German Romantic philosophy and how it contributed to defining the era, which will be useful for students of philosophy, aesthetics, and literature.

Feldman, Paula R., and Theresa M. Kelley, eds. *Romantic Women Writers Voices and Countervoices*. Hanover, NH: University Press of New England, 1995. This anthology includes articles on Mary Shelley, Lætitia Barbauld, Felicia Hemans, and Joanna Baillie and describes their various forms of artistic expression.

Furst, Lilian. *Romanticism in Perspective: A Comparative Study of Aspects of Romantic Movements in England, France, and Germany*. 1969. Reprint. London: Macmillan, 1972. This readable work examines some of Romanticism's most important themes including individualism, imagination, feeling, and the concept of the Romantic hero.

Hayter, Althea. *Opium and the Romantic Imagination*. Los Angeles: University of California Press, 1968. This work discusses the historical use of opium and its frequency among Romantic writers. She dismisses the idea that authors were "high" when they wrote their best poetry.

Kelly, Catriona. *A History of Russian Women's Writing, 1820–1992*. New York: Oxford University Press, 1994. Divided by historical era, Kelly introduces each period and then the prominent writers, including Karolina Pavlova and several others active during the Romantic era.

Larmore, Charles. *The Romantic Legacy*. New York: Columbia University Press, 1996. This work discusses Romanticism's legacy and addresses A. O. Lovejoy's initial question about the difficulty of defining Romanticism.

McFarland, Thomas. *Romanticism and the Heritage of Rousseau*. Oxford: Clarendon Press, 1995. An important discussion which relates Rousseau to the British Romantics.

Mellor, Anne K., ed. *Romanticism and Feminism*. Bloomington: Indiana University Press, 1988. This collection of essays analyzes Romantic texts from a feminist perspective.

————. *Romanticism and Gender*. New York: Routledge, 1993. This work discusses five British men Romantics and then investigates how topics, styles, and focus change when women authors and their works are interpreted.

Murray, Christopher John, ed. *Encyclopedia of the Romantic Era*. 2 vols. Chicago: Fitzroy-Dearborn, 2003. Masterful reference work that contains 770 articles about the Romantic Era, primarily focusing on western Europe, Great Britain, and the United States.

Oerlemans, Onno. *Romanticism and the Materiality of Nature*. Buffalo, NY: University of Toronto Press, 2002. This study examines the Romantic attachment to nature and includes discussions of among others Wordsworth and Shelley and their views about the environment.

Peckham, Morse. *The Birth of Romanticism, 1790–1815*. Greenwood, FL: Penkeville Publishing Co., 1986. This book provides an accessible thematic discussion of European Romanticism and the related writers, artists, and musicians. It also explores Romanticism's link to Modernism.

Prawer, Siegbert, ed. *The Romantic Period in Germany: Essays by Members of the London University Institute of Germanic Studies*. New York: Schocken Books, 1970. These essays explore German Romanticism from the perspective of literary genres, philosophy, music, and painting.

Riasonovsky, Nicholas. *The Emergence of Romanticism*. New York: Oxford University Press, 1992. Noted Russian historian discusses Romanticism in England and Germany and its links to pantheism.

Richards, Robert. *The Romantic Conception of Life Science and Philosophy in the Age of Goethe*. Chicago: University of Chicago Press, 2002. This interesting book discusses Goethe, the Schlegels, and other German Romantics, and their philosophical relationship to science, especially biology, and the resulting legacy to modern science.

Richardson, Alan. *Literature, Education and Romanticism: Reading as Social Practice, 1780–1832*. Cambridge: Cambridge University Press, 1994.

The work investigates schooling and literacy in Britain from 1780 to 1832, using Romantic texts from Rousseau, Blake, Wordsworth, and Mary Shelley, to discuss pedagogical method, children's literature, and women's education among other subjects.

Roe, Nicholas, ed. *Romanticism: An Oxford Guide*. New York: Oxford University Press, 2005. The volume contains forty-six essays on various aspects of British Romanticism and articles about environmentalism, modernism, postmodernism, and the like. Essays, while written by experts, are accessible and provide bibliographical references.

Schenk, H. G. *The Mind of the European Romantics*. Garden City, NY: Doubleday/Anchor, 1969. This is an older but nevertheless serviceable survey of European Romanticism.

Teich, Mikulá, and Roy Porter, eds. *Romanticism in National Context*. New York: Cambridge University Press, 1993. This collection of essays discusses the rise of nationalism in various European nations, including lesser-known manifestations in places like the Netherlands, Sweden, and Hungary.

Todd, Janet. *The Sign of Angellica Women, Writing and Fiction, 1660–1800*. New York: Columbia University Press, 1989. This work examines British women writers against the context of their time. Part Three focuses on women associated with the Age of Romanticism, including Frances Burney and Ann Radcliffe.

Walzel, Oscar. *German Romanticism*. Translated by Alma Elsie Lussky. 1932. Reprint. New York: Capricorn Books, 1966. This older work provides a readable and balanced overview of German Romantic writers and their works. It serves as a solid introduction for the nonexpert.

Wu, Duncan, ed. *A Companion to Romanticism*. Malden, MA: Blackwell, 2001. A compendium of essays that explores historical background, genres, and debates surrounding Romanticism. It also includes comments on various primary sources, with works of British Romanticism predominating.

Poets and Poetry

Bentley, G. E., Jr. *The Stranger from Paradise: A Biography of William Blake*. New Haven, CT: Yale University Press, 2001. Respected Blake scholar has produced this massive volume exploring the man, his writings, his art, and his eccentric genius.

Bone, Drummond, ed. *The Cambridge Companion to Byron*. New York: Cambridge University Press, 2004. A rich collection of sixteen essays meant for teachers and students alike, which explores Byron, his literary output, his travels, and how the rest of Europe reacted to him.

Cox, Jeffrey. _Poetry and Politics in the Cockney School: Keats, Shelley, Hunt, and Their Circle._ Cambridge Studies in Romanticism. Cambridge: Cambridge University Press, 2004. An interesting study of the second generation of British Romantics and their reactions to their time.

Eaves, Morris, ed. _The Cambridge Companion to William Blake._ New York: Cambridge University Press, 2003. This collection of thirteen scholarly articles provides a broad overview of Blake, his writings, and engravings.

Fletcher, Pauline, and John Murphy, eds. _Wordsworth in Context._ Lewisburg, PA: Bucknell University Press, 1992. The work contains essays that discuss the political context of William's writing and Dorothy and her poetry.

Gill, Steven, ed. _The Cambridge Companion to William Wordsworth._ New York: Cambridge University Press, 2003. This collection of fourteen essays provides a solid entrée for students to the life and work of William Wordsworth and his many poetic achievements.

Gilmour, Ian. _The Making of the Poets: Byron and Shelley and Their Time._ New York: Carroll and Graf, 2004. This readable and entertaining work presents a dual biography of the formative years of the two famous poets.

Greene, Diana. _Reinventing Romantic Poetry: Russian Women Poets of the Mid-Nineteenth Century._ Madison: University of Wisconsin Press, 2003. The work compares fourteen men and fourteen women poets active in mid-nineteenth century Russia. It argues that women poets had to search for different muses than the men.

Greenleaf, Monika. _Pushkin and Romantic Fashion: Fragment, Elegy, Orient, Irony._ Stanford, CA: Stanford University Press, 1995. A landmark study of Pushkin, his life, and work—a sophisticated but clear discussion.

Holmes, Richard. _Coleridge: Darker Reflections, 1804–1834._ New York: Pantheon Books, 1999. This is the second volume of the Holmes's biography of Coleridge.

———. _Coleridge: Early Visions, 1772–1804._ 1990. Reprint. New York: Pantheon Books, 1999. This is the first volume of a massive biography of Coleridge that gets beyond the drug addiction, financial woes, and suspected plagiarism to examine this man from all sides.

Homans, Margaret. _Women Writers and Poetic Identity: Dorothy Wordsworth, Emily Brontë, and Emily Dickinson._ Princeton, NJ: Princeton University Press, 1980. One of the earliest literary/historical studies to discuss women who wrote poetry during the Age of Romanticism, which explores their isolation in a field dominated by men.

Johnston, Kenneth. _The Hidden Wordsworth: Poet, Lover, Rebel, Spy._ New York: W. W. Norton, 1998. In this massive study, Johnston investigates minutiae about Wordsworth's life in an attempt to fill in the missing details about the poet, especially the decade of the 1790s.

Jones, Kathleen. *Sisterhood: Women of the Wordsworth Circle.* New York: St. Martin's Press, 2000. Interesting discussion of the wives, sisters, and daughters of the Wordsworth circle and how these women contributed to maintaining this vibrant intellectual group.

Matlak, Richard. *The Poetry of Relationship: The Wordsworths and Coleridge.* New York: St. Martin's Press, 1997. This psychobiography examines the personal interaction among Dorothy Wordsworth, William Wordsworth, and Samuel Taylor Coleridge. It deviates from older studies by exploring Dorothy's role in this friendship more fully and also her influence on her brother's poetry.

McGann, Jerome J. *The Romantic Ideology: A Critical Investigation.* Chicago: University of Chicago Press, 1983. This close examination of Wordsworth, Coleridge, Shelley, and Lord Byron suggests that their poetry cannot be understood without the historical context.

Morton, Timothy, and Marilyn Butler. *Shelley and the Revolution in Taste: The Body and the Natural World.* New York: Cambridge University Press, 1995. This study seriously investigates Shelley's commitment to vegetarianism and how his attitudes about food and drink emerge from his writings.

Motion, Andrew. *Keats.* Chicago: University of Chicago Press, 1999. This lengthy biography of Keats provides a thoughtful discussion of the man and his times, accessible to the nonscholar.

Newlyn, Lucy, ed. *The Cambridge Companion to Coleridge.* New York: Cambridge University Press, 2002. This collection of fifteen essays explores Coleridge's literary works, his autobiography, and his critical and journalistic efforts.

Ross, Marlon B. *The Contours of Masculine Desire: Romanticism and the Rise of Women's Poetry.* New York: Oxford University Press, 1989. This work, path-breaking when it appeared, looks at gender's role in poetry—that is, how it is read, written, published, and reviewed.

Sweet, Nanora, and Julie Melynyk, eds. *Felicia Hemans: Reimagining Poetry in the Nineteenth Century.* New York: Palgrave, 2001. This anthology presents twelve essays that explore aspects of Hemans's life and poetry. The introduction explains the surge in interest in Hemans and her poetry.

Unger, Richard. *Hölderlin's Major Poetry: The Dialectics of Unity.* Bloomington: Indiana University Press, 1975. This offers criticism and interpretation of Hölderlin's poetry and also presents the poems in German and English translation.

Vincent, Patrick H. *The Romantic Poetess: European Culture, Politics, and Gender, 1820–1840.* Durham, NH: University of New England Press, 2004. This study examines women poets from England to Russia and describes how their works relate to those of Madame de Staël and share commonalities regarding the place of the woman poet in European society and politics.

Wolfson, Susan J., ed. *The Cambridge Companion to John Keats.* New York: Cambridge University Press, 2001. The fifteen essays discuss Keats, his life, his poetry and letters, the Cockney school, and the politics of his poetry.

Wu, Duncan. *Wordsworth: An Inner Life.* Cambridge, MA: Blackwell, 2002. Wordsworth's early life experiences, such as the loss of his parents as a young child, are examined and used to help explore some of his poetry.

Novels, Dramas, Nonfiction, and Their Authors

Boyle, Nicholas. *Goethe: The Poet and the Age.* Vol. 1, *The Poetry of Desire, 1749–1790.* New York: Oxford University Press, 1992. The definitive and accessible biography of Goethe in English places him in the midst of the intellectual milieu of his time.

————. *Goethe: The Poet and the Age.* Vol. 2, *Revolution and Renunciation, 1790–1803.* New York: Oxford University Press, 2003. This second installment of the Boyle biography is regarded as a major contribution to literary and historical scholarship.

Clarke, Norma. *Ambitious Heights: Writing, Friendship and Love: The Jewsbury Sisters, Felicia Hemans, and Jane Welsh Carlyle.* New York: Routledge, 1990. This study discusses these women and their friendships and how their commitment to writing, as a profession, challenged women's traditional domestic role.

Copeland, Edward, and Juliet McMaster, eds. *The Cambridge Companion to Jane Austen.* New York: Cambridge University Press, 1997. These twelve essays discuss Austen's life, her fiction, her letters, as well as themes that appear in her works.

Cox, Jeffrey. *In the Shadows of Romance: Romantic Tragic Drama in Germany, England, and France.* Athens: Ohio University Press, 1987. This work examines the dramas of several well-known figures of the Age of Romanticism, including Goethe, Shelley, Byron, and others.

Dabundo, Laura, ed. *Jane Austen and Mary Shelley and Their Sisters.* New York: University Press of America, 2000. A collection of readable essays, which introduce British women novelists and their works.

Damrosch, Leo. *Jean-Jacques Rousseau: Restless Genius.* Boston: Houghton-Mifflin, 2005. Most recent and readable biography of Rousseau, which despite its positive bias about him, presents insightful interpretations of the man and his writings.

Dekker, George G. *The Fictions of Romantic Tourism: Radcliffe, Scott and Mary Shelley.* Stanford: Stanford University Press, 2004. The work describes how these authors' travels affected the novels that they wrote.

Duncan, Ian. *Modern Romance and Transformation of the Novel: The Gothic, Scott, Dickens.* Cambridge: Cambridge University Press, 1995. This work discusses how Gothic romance sets the stage for modern prose fiction, which becomes standardized in the Waverley novels of Sir Walter Scott and then the works of Charles Dickens.

Ellis, Kate Ferguson. *The Contested Castle: Gothic Novels and the Subversion of Domestic Ideology.* Chicago: University of Illinois Press, 1989. This book discusses the evolution of Gothic novels, highlighting those of Horace Walpole, Clara Reeve, Ann Radcliffe, and Mary Shelley among others.

Ferris, Ina. *The Achievement of Literary Authority: Gender, History and the Waverley Novels.* Ithaca, NY: Cornell University Press, 1991. An interesting discussion of Sir Walter Scott's novels explores the relationship between the "national tales" and the historical novel in Great Britain.

Gillespie, Gerald, ed. *Romantic Drama.* A Comparative History of Literature in European Languages, Vol. 9. Philadelphia: John Benjamins Publishing Co., 1994. This work contains twenty-six essays on Romantic-era drama ranging across Europe.

Halsall, Albert W. *Victor Hugo and the Romantic Drama.* Toronto: University of Toronto Press, 1998. This work presents a careful study of the man, his dramas, and his contribution to the Romantic theater.

Herold, J. Christopher. *Mistress to an Age: A Life of Madame de Staël.* 1958. Reprint. New York: Crown Publishers, Harmony Books, 1979. A biography of this prominent historical figure, which provides a solid introduction for the nonspecialist.

Heyden, John O., ed. *Scott: The Critical Heritage.* New York: Barnes and Noble, 1970. A collection of critical essays that review Scott's works.

Hoeveler, Diane Long. *Gothic Feminism: The Professionalization of Gender from Charlotte Smith to the Brontës.* University Park: Pennsylvania State University Press, 1998. This presents a modern literary analysis of Gothic novels and their authors, discussing the stereotypes that have emerged from the genre and exploring the construct of gender.

Hogle, Jerrold, ed. *The Cambridge Companion to Gothic Fiction.* New York: Cambridge University Press, 2002. These fourteen essays discuss Gothic fiction from the eighteenth through the twentieth centuries. Six essays focus on the Gothic and the Age of Romanticism.

Johnson, Claudia L. *Jane Austen: Women, Politics and the Novel.* Chicago: University of Chicago Press, 1988. This work examines Austen's skepticism about her society and how she uses the family in her novels as a paradigm for the state.

Levin, Susan. *Dorothy Wordsworth and Romanticism.* New Brunswick, NJ: Rutgers University Press, 1987. This study offers an accessible literary discussion of Dorothy's writing. It also includes all of Dorothy's known poems.

Morrison, Lucy, and Staci L. Stone. *A Mary Shelley Encyclopedia*. Westport, CT: Greenwood Press, 2003. An up-to-date reference work, it highlights Mary Shelley's lesser known works as well as *Frankenstein*.

Morse, David. *Romanticism: A Structural Analysis*. Totowa, NJ: Barnes and Noble, 1982. This work discusses the genres of Romantic literature, including the *Märchen*, the Gothic and historical novels, and historic drama.

Norton, Rictor. *Mistress of Udolfo: The Life of Ann Radcliffe*. New York: Leicester University Press, 1999. The most recent biography of Radcliffe dispels the myths about her insanity and sequestration late in life.

Robb, Graham. *Victor Hugo*. New York: W. W. Norton, 1998. Lengthy but very readable biography of Hugo describes his well-known and not so well-known works.

Schor, Ester, ed. *The Cambridge Companion to Mary Shelley*. New York: Cambridge University Press, 2003. The collection of sixteen essays examines Mary Shelley, in light of new literary and historical approaches to her and her works.

Seymour, Miranda. *Mary Shelley*. London: John Murray, 2000. A nuanced portrait of Mary Shelley that reveals her multiple sides, including her detestation of slavery and her active literary life after *Frankenstein*.

Sharpe, Lesley, ed. *The Cambridge Companion to Goethe*. New York: Cambridge University Press, 2002. This collection of fifteen essays discusses the noted author, his literary, autobiographical, and scientific works, and his world at the Weimar court.

Thalmann, Marianne. *The Romantic Fairy Tale: Seeds of Surrealism*. Translated by Mary B. Corcoran. Ann Arbor: University of Michigan Press, 1964. This work discusses the *Märchen* in German Romanticism and highlights Ludwig Tieck's contributions.

Williams, John. *Mary Shelley: A Literary Life*. New York: St. Martin's Press, 2000. Balanced discussion of Mary Shelley's stormy life, which moves beyond *Frankenstein* to her lesser known works.

Winegarten, Renee. *Madame de Staël*. Dover, NH: Berg Publishers, 1987. Brief biography of de Staël, meant for the nonspecialist, which discusses her life and importance to her times.

Art and Artists

Brown, David Blayney. *Romanticism*. New York: Phaidon Press, 2001. This is a well-written discussion of Romanticism and the related great works of art.

Jensen, Jens Christian. *Caspar David Friedrich*. Translated by Joachim Neugroschel. Woodbury, NY: Barron's, 1981. This is a succinct and well-written biography of this eminent German Romantic painter.

Rodner, William S. *J. M. W. Turner: Romantic Painter of the Industrial Revolution*. Berkeley: University of California Press, 1997. Discusses Turner's "industrial art" and how he examined the juxtaposition of steam power and the environment.

Sala, Charles. *Caspar David Friedrich and Romantic Painting*. Paris: Terrail, 1994. The work discusses Friedrich's life and paintings and also his relationship to other Romantic artists, including J. M. W. Turner and John Constable. It includes one hundred reproductions.

Townsend, Joyce H., ed. *William Blake: The Painter at Work*. Princeton, NJ: Princeton University Press, 2004. A collection of essays which explores Blake's unique methods and style and reproduces many of his works, in color and black and white.

Vaughan, William. *Romanticism and Art*. New York: Thames and Hudson, 1994. Very accessible survey of the art works of the era, with numerous reproductions.

Music and Composers

Blume, Friedrich. *Classic and Romantic Music: A Comprehensive Survey*. Translated by M. D. Herter Norton. New York: W. W. Norton, 1970. This nontechnical introduction sets Classical and Romantic music within a historical context.

Glickman, Sylvia, and Martha Furman Schleifer, eds. *From Convent to Concert Hall: A Guide to Women Composers*. Westport, CT: Greenwood Press, 2003. This work introduces women composers, including Clara Wieck Schumann, involved with Western music since the ninth century.

Hanning, Barbara Russano. *Concise History of Western Music*. New York: W. W. Norton, 1998. This is a clearly presented revision of an older history of music. It provides a basic introduction to the eras, the major composers, and orchestral and musical innovations.

Köhler, Joachim. *Richard Wagner: The Last of the Titans*. Translated by Stewart Spencer. New Haven, CT: Yale University Press, 2004. A well-researched biography of Wagner which investigates many of his personal relationships and how they affected his views about love, death, and nationalism.

Lockwood, Lewis. *Beethoven: The Music and the Life*. 2002. Reprint. New York: W. W. Norton, 2005. This accessible biography discusses Beethoven in terms of the three musical periods in his life and emphasizes the influence of Classical composers.

Raeburn, Michael, and Alan Kendall, eds. *Heritage of Music: The Romantic Era*. Vol. II. New York: Oxford University Press, 1989. This work offers a readable overview of composers' lives, their times, and instruments used.

Rosen, Charles. *The Romantic Generation.* Cambridge, MA: Harvard, 1995. This work provides a densely written treatment of the era with particular attention to Schumann, Mendelssohn, Berlioz, and Chopin.

Schonberg, Harold C. *The Lives of the Great Composers.* 3rd ed. New York: W. W. Norton, 1997. This is a collection of readable biographical sketches of the great composers and their contributions.

Siepmann, Jeremy. *Chopin: The Reluctant Romantic.* Boston: Northeastern University Press, 1995. This work is an enjoyable biography of the man and his music.

Walker, Alan. *Franz Liszt.* 3 vols. New York: Knopf, Random House, 1983–1996. This multivolume work is the definitive biography of this great composer and musician.

Whittall, Arnold. *Romantic Music: A Concise History from Schubert to Sibelius.* New York: Thames and Hudson, 1987. The discussion focuses on well-known Romantic composers across Europe and their music, and how its expressiveness makes it recognizably Romantic.

Web Sites

Bibliography of German Romantic Literary Criticism and Theory in English (http://www.highbeam.com/library Keyword: German Romanticism) Provides essays about aspects of German Romanticism and its practitioners.

Blake Archive. Edited by Morris Eaves, Robert Essick, and Joseph Visconti (http://www.blakearchive.org) Contains copies of Blake's illustrated books, including text and annotations.

British Women Romantic Poets, 1789–1832. Shields Library, University of California, Davis (http://digital.lib.ucdavis.edu/projects/bwrp/BWRP) Contains fifty books of poetry, many unpublished since the Romantic era of works written by seventy-six English and Irish authors.

English Romantic Literature Subject Guide. Edited by Patrick L. Carr (http://www.lib.rochester.edu/index) Organized by type of source, such as encyclopedias, companion guides, literary criticism (Romantic-era and modern authors), bibliographies, manuscripts, and websites among others. Complete with annotations, this site provides a useful tool for anyone interested in the English Romantics. (Last updated 7/6/06.)

Literary Resources on the Net—Romanticism. Edited by Jack Lynch (http://andromeda.rutgers.edu/~jlynch/Lit/romantic) Extensive list of primary and secondary sources including scholarly journals associated with Romantic literature.

Project Gutenberg (http://promo.net/pg/) Extensive collection of primary sources, begun in 1971, including many great Romantic-era works.

Romantic Circles. Edited by Neil Fraistat, Steven E. Jones, and Carl Stahmer (http://www.rc.umd.edu) This is a particularly important site for the study of the later Romantics.

Romanticism on the Net (http://www.ron.umontreal) Online journal that focuses on Romanticism and includes articles, book reviews, and links to current Internet sites.

Romantic Links, Electronic Texts and Home Pages. Edited by Michael Gamer (http://www.english.upenn.edu/~mgamer/Romantic) This site provides electronic links for the British Romantics grouped according to subject: General Literary Sites, Romanticist Associations, Romantic Sites, Author Sites, Electronic Texts, and Romanticists' Home Pages.

Voice of the Shuttle Web Site for Humanities Research: Romanticism (http://vos.uscb.edu) The listing of Internet resources on Romanticism includes references to such things as general sources, the North American Society for the Study of Romanticism, Romantic Circles, Romantic Anthologies, Romanticism on the Net, Authors, Works, and ongoing research.

CD-ROMs and DVDs

Batavick, Frank, and Victor Font. *Romanticism: Imagining Freedom*. [DVD] (2005). Princeton, NJ: Films for the Humanities and Sciences. This explores Romantic themes such as nature, love, and death in literature, painting, and music. It highlights the works of Wordsworth, Byron, Keats, Hölderlin, Turner, and Beethoven.

Beethoven: The Age of Revolution. [DVD] (1988, 2002). Princeton, NJ: Films for the Humanities. This documents Beethoven's life and work until 1804 and relates its evolution against the backdrop of the French Revolution.

Chancellor, Anne, and Nicky Patterson. *The Real Jane Austen*. [DVD] (2002, 2004). Princeton, NJ: Films for the Humanities and Sciences. This provides a biographical and psychological profile of Jane Austen set against the expectations associated with a woman's life in late eighteenth and early nineteenth century Britain.

Chang, Liz, Tony Middleton, Pablo Garcia, and Fernanda Dominguez. *Victor Hugo*. [DVD] (2004). Princeton, NJ: Films for the Humanities. This Tranquilo Producciones work explores Victor Hugo and his life. It contrasts his humble beginnings and his political stances against his status as one of France's literary giants.

Collier, Adeline, Kevin Marsland, Rod Smith, Hugh Dickson, and David March. *Poetry of Landscape: William Wordsworth and the English Lakes*. [DVD] (2005). Princeton, NJ: Films for the Humanities and Sciences.

The production, done on behalf of the British Tourist Authority, describes the Lake District, from which Wordsworth and many British Romantic poets drew their inspiration.

Cox, Brian, János Darvas, and Jane Lapotaire. *Johannes Brahms: But for women* .... [DVD] (1996, 2003). Princeton, NJ: Films for the Humanities and Sciences. This work, originally produced by Metropolitan München in association with Westdeutscher Rundfunk Köln in 1996, explores the life and work of Brahms.

Downes, Mary, and Robert Winston. *Mary Shelley: The Birth of Frankenstein.* [DVD] (2004). Princeton, NJ: Films for the Humanities and Sciences. This reissue of a BBC broadcast from 2003 explores how aspects of Mary Shelley's life influenced the creation of her famous novel.

English Poetry Anthology—The Romantic Poets. [DVD] (2006). West Long Branch, NJ: Kultur International Films. First produced in 1999 as *The Romantic Poets* on videodisc, this Cromwell Productions presentation discusses the five prominent British Romantic poets and interprets some of their well-known works.

The English Poets [CD-ROM]. (n.d.) Princeton, NJ: Films for the Humanities. This source provides information on the five well-known British Romantic poets and John Clare. It contains biographies of the men, their wives, and other friends who influenced them. It has an extensive bibliography.

Galway, James, and Derek Bailey. *Music in Time, Part 11: Nationalism and Revolution.* [DVD] (1982, 2003). Princeton, NJ: Films for the Humanities. This work examines various composers against the background of the political events which affected their decisions to rely on folk themes and incorporate nationalist sentiments. The composers discussed include Berlioz, Liszt, Wagner, and Verdi.

————. *Music in Time, Part 13: The Mighty Fistful—Russian Composers.* [DVD] (2003). Princeton, NJ: Films for the Humanities. This work explores how Russian audiences, who had preferred European music in the nineteenth century, came to appreciate the music of Glinka and others, who based their work on Russian folktales.

Galway, James, Derek Bailey, and James Archibald. *Music in Time, Part 10: The Romantics.* [DVD] (2003). Princeton, NJ: Films for the Humanities and Sciences. This addresses the theme of self-expression so important to the Romantics. The compositions of Brahms, Chopin, Mendelssohn, and Schumann are highlighted.

Gascoigne, Bamber, and Tony Cash. *Schubert: The Young Romantic.* [DVD] (1987, 2003). Princeton, NJ: Films for the Humanities. Originally produced by Granada Television International in 1986, this film explores the life and works of Franz Schubert.

Greenberg, Robert, Tamara Stonebarger, and Tom Dunton. *Great Masters Liszt and His Music*. [DVD] (2002). Chantilly, VA: Teaching Co. In eight lectures, the life and work of Franz Liszt are explored.

Jean-Jacques Rousseau: Retreat to Romanticism. [DVD] (2004). Princeton, NJ: Films for the Humanities and Sciences. This reissue of a 1991 project by Open University, British Broadcasting Corporation, describes the life and thought of Rousseau. It emphasizes Rousseau's critique of contemporary French society and the ideas that tie him to the Romantics, such as love of nature and individual freedom.

Kogosowski, Alan, and Paul Barton. *Frederic Chopin: A Life to Remember*. [DVD] (2003) Special Edition. Australia: Edit 1 Video Productions. This documentary traces the life and works of Chopin.

The Lake Poets. [DVD] (2003). Princeton, NJ: Films for the Humanities. This explores the lives of William Wordsworth and Samuel Taylor Coleridge and their literary development.

Landmarks of Western Art: A Journey of Art History over the Ages: Romanticism. [DVD] (2006). West Long Branch, NJ: Kultur International Films. Art historians analyze the important artists associated with the Age of Romanticism, including Turner, Constable, Friedrich, Géricault, and Delacroix among others.

The Last Journey of John Keats. [DVD] (2002). Princeton, NJ: Films for the Humanities and Sciences. Keats's biographer Andrew Motion provides a realistic portrait of Keats, enhanced by quotations from his poems and letters, which traces his travels in Italy as he sought a cure for his tuberculosis.

Manson, David, Lara Lowe, and Tim Morton. *Romanticism*. [DVD] (1999). West Long Branch, NJ: Kultur International Films. Select art historians describe Romanticism's impact on the development of art in the Western World, including the works of Turner, Constable, and Géricault.

Perkins, Jack, Ron Perlman, Bruce Koken, Michael White, Robert Greenberg, and Richard Gibb. *Beethoven: The Sound and the Fury*. [DVD] (2004). Burlington, VT: A & E Home Video. From the acclaimed A & E Biography series, this examines Beethoven's life, personal triumphs and failures, and his tortured genius.

Persisting Dreams: Byron's Romanticism. [DVD] (2002). Princeton, NJ: Films for the Humanities and Sciences. This reissue of a BBC production from 1996 explores Byron's life in Venice and how his work influenced other Romantics, including the French painter Eugène Delacroix.

Pioneers of the Spirit: William Blake. [DVD] (2005). Worcester, PA: Vision Video. This biographical study discusses Blake as poet, engraver, painter, and visionary as a means to explore his "inner world" and reveals the insights he has left for posterity.

Romanticism: The CD-ROM. Edited by David S. Miall and Duncan Wu (http://www.ualberta.ca/~dmiall/romancdinf.htm) This CD comes with *Romanticism: An Anthology,* ed. Duncan Wu (Oxford: Blackwell, 1997). It contains documents, prints, and photographs relating to the era.

Russell, Ken, and Melvyn Bragg. *"The Rime of the Ancient Mariner": The Strange Story of Samuel Taylor Coleridge, Poet and Drug Addict.* [DVD] (2003). Princeton, NJ: Films for the Humanities and Sciences. This explores Coleridge's unhappy life and intertwines themes from the poem and how they relate to the poet's story.

Wordsworth's "Spots of Time." [DVD] (2003). Princeton, NJ: Films for the Humanities and Sciences. This work, filmed in the Lake District, follows William Wordsworth's life and uses references to his major poem *The Prelude* throughout to explore his key ideas about the poet and his imagination.

INDEX

About the Author

JOANNE SCHNEIDER is an associate professor of history and current department chair at Rhode Island College in Providence, Rhode Island. She is co-editor of *Women in Western European History* (Greenwood, 1986). She is currently working on a project involving welfare and religion in Bavaria from 1790 to 1830.